33 Cycle
in Northumberland & Tyneside

Weetwood Bridge, Route 11. Photo: © Andy McCandlish/www.andymccandlish.com

Compiled by Ted Liddle

First published in the United Kingdom in 2017 by Northern Heritage Services Limited
2nd edition - updated and published 2019

Northern Heritage Services Limited
Units 7&8 New Kennels, Blagdon Estate, Seaton Burn,
Newcastle upon Tyne NE13 6DB
Telephone: 01670 789 940
www.northern-heritage.co.uk

See our full online catalogue at www.northern-heritage.co.uk

Text copyright:
© 2016 Ted Liddle

Edited by:
Dr Máire West

Photographs not otherwise attributed:
© 2016 Ted Liddle

Design and layout:
© 2016 Ian Scott Design

Ordnance Survey Map Data 1:50 000 scale
2cm to 1 km - 1 1/4 Inches to 1 mile

© Crown Copyright 2016 Licence No 100056069

Printed and bound in UK by Webmart UK

British Library Cataloguing in Publishing Data
A catalogue record for this book is available from the British Library.

ISBN 978-0-9931161-4-8

MIX
Paper from responsible sources
FSC® C146037

All rights reserved.
No part of this book may be reproduced, stored or introduced into a retrieval system, or transmitted in any form or by any means (electronic, mechanical, photocopying, recording or otherwise) without the prior permission of the publisher.

Ted mountain biking above Zermatt, Switzerland.

Ted Liddle

Ted Liddle is an enthusiastic mountain biker and road cyclist. He has extensive knowledge, not only of the huge number of minor roads and the off-road network of rights of way and trails in the north of England, but also parts of Scotland and of many areas of the Alps.

Since 1994, Ted has devised some 2,000 miles of cycle routes in the north of England, many of which are mapped and signed. He has suggested countless loops, both on and off-road. His specialism is creating high-quality, long-distance cycle routes, including the challenging 120-mile-long mostly off-road Sandstone Way in Northumberland **www.sandstoneway.co.uk**. There are more route developments in the pipeline including **www.reiverscycleroute.co.uk**.

Ted has compiled 24 cycle route maps and guides and is the author of three guidebooks, with several more in progress. Recreational cycling and the dynamics of cycle tourism are two of his key strengths but Ted is also well known for his advocacy of, and advisory work on, all aspects of cycling.

Ted is a regional Cycling UK Right to Ride representative and North-East regional contact for OpenMTB, the new national voice for mountain biking. He is also chairman of Tyne Valley MTB Cycling Club. **www.tynevalleymtbcycling.co.uk**

19 Denotes route no. and where the route starts
20 BERWICK-UPON-TWEED
Spittal
Goswick
Cheswick
Holy Island
(Lindisfarne)
West Mains
Coldstream
Etal
Heatherslaw
Ford
Lowick
BAMBURGH
Farne Islands
Mindrum
12 Milfield
BELFORD 9
Doddington
10 8 SEAHOUSES
19
Lucker
WOOLER 11 21
Chatton
Lilburn
Craster
ALNWICK
ALNMOUTH
Shilbottle
6 7 WARKWORTH
18
Amble
22 ROTHBURY
NORTH SEA
Widdrington
Widdrington Station
13 14 KIELDER
Otterburn
Ulgham
Kielder Water
Woodhorn 8
Cresswell
Falstone
2
5
Hartburn
Mitford
3
33 ASHINGTON
MORPETH
4
BELLINGHAM
Bedlington
BLYTH
32
CRAMLINGTON
Wark
New Hartley
Seaton Sluice
PONTELAND
KILLINGWORTH
Backworth
31 WHITLEY BAY
25
28
Matfen
16
Woolsington
Wideopen
29
Cullercoats
Stamfordham
Shiremoor
30 TYNEMOUTH
Heddon-on-the-Wall
Throckley
North Shields
HALTWHISTLE
Haydon Bridge
27 Wallsend
Bardon Mill
HEXHAM 15
Corbridge
Wylam 1
23 26
NEWCASTLE-UPON-TYNE
17
24
Newburn
PRUDHOE
GATESHEAD
ALLENDALE

Routes featured

Ride Number and title	Page	Distance	Grade
CYCLE RIDES ON-ROAD			
1. Wylam & Matfen Loop	17	46.2 km / 29 miles	Moderate
2. Morpeth & Whalton Loop	21	34 km / 21.25 miles	Moderate
3. Morpeth & Hartburn Loop	24	40 km / 25 miles	Moderate
4. Morpeth & Ulgham Loop	27	33.5 km / 21 miles	Moderate
5. Cresswell, Coast & Inland Loop	30	29.4km / 18.4 miles	Moderate
6. Warkworth & Shilbottle Loop	33	24.75 km /15.5 miles	Moderate
7. Warkworth & Alnmouth Loop	36	14.25 km / 9 miles	Easy
8. Alnmouth to Bamburgh Linear	38	43.6 km / 27.25 miles	Easy
9. Belford, Chatton & Lowick Loop	43	41 km / 25.6 miles	Moderate
10. Seahouses, Bamburgh & Lucker Loop	47	29 km / 18 miles	Easy
11. Wooler, Heatherslaw & Lowick Loop	50	45.4 km / 28.4 miles	Moderate
12. Milfield, Heatherslaw & Mindrum Loop	55	35 km / 22 miles	Moderate
CYCLE RIDES BY MTB - MOUNTAIN BIKE			
13. Kielder Water Lakeside Way Loop	61	39 km / 24.5 miles	Moderate
14. The Osprey: Kielder Loop	64	20.5 km / 12.7 miles	Moderate
15. Hexham, Acomb & St Oswald's Loop	66	12.3 km / 7.5 miles	Moderate
16. The Stamfordham & Matfen Loop	68	27.75 km / 17 miles	Easy
17. Prudhoe & Heddon-on-the-Wall Loop	71	27 km / 17 miles	Moderate
18. Warkworth & the Coast Loop	74	17 km / 10.6 miles	Easy
19. Seahouses & Bamburgh	76	20.35 km / 12.7 miles	Easy
20. Berwick-upon-Tweed to Holy Island Linear	79	17 km / 10.6 miles	Easy
21. Wooler & Lilburn Tower Loop	83	17 km / 10.6 miles	Moderate
22. Rothbury & Great Tosson MTB Loop	86	11 km / 7 miles	Easy/Moderate
WAGGONWAYS & BRIDLEWAYS			
23. Wylam & Newburn Rail Path Loop	91	19 km / 11.9 miles	Easy
24. Wylam & Newburn Upper Loop	94	21.6 km / 13.5 miles	Easy
25. Ponteland & Heddon-on-the-Wall Loop	97	28 km / 18 miles	Moderate
26. Throckley Dene & Woolsington Figure of Eight	100	16.4 km / 10 miles	Moderate
27. Newcastle & North Tyneside Loop	102	27 km / 17 miles	Moderate
28. Killingworth & Gosforth Loop	105	23.4 km / 14.6 miles	Easy
29. Cramlington & Backworth Loop	108	31.75 km / 20 miles	Easy
30. Tynemouth, Coast & Inland Loop	111	25.75 km / 16 miles	Easy
31. Whitley Bay & New Hartley Loop	115	16.7 km / 10.5 miles	Easy
32. Blyth & Seaton Sluice Loop	118	27.5 km / 17.2 miles	Easy
33. Ashington & River Wansbeck Loop	121	6.6 km / 10.3 miles	Easy

Legend

CYCLE ROUTE INFORMATION

Short Cut

Road Routes

Off-highway verge path, family-friendly section - suitable for road bikes

Road section - take extra care crossing

Main road section - take extra care when riding here

Family-friendly sections or entire route - suitable for road bikes

Mountain Bike MTB Routes

Short cut

Waggonway / Bridleway Route

Short cut

Recommended direction of travel

Route bi-directional

National Cycle Network (NCN)

1	🚴	National Cycle Network route number
1		Coasts & Castles Cycle Route
68		Pennine Cycleway
76		Round The Forth Cycle Route
10		Reivers Cycle Route
72		Hadrian's Cycleway

• • ● NCN on-road

° ° ○ NCN off-road

ROADS & PATHS

A1 Unfenced Trunk Road — Dual Carriageway

A6105 Main Road

B6354 Secondary Road

Other Road

Stone-based farm road/track

Bridge Bridge Gate/Cattle-grid

Steep hill

Footpath

Bridleway

Restricted Byway (not for use by mechanically propelled vehicles)

Byway open to all traffic

Other route with public access

Path

National trail, long-distance footpath

Railways

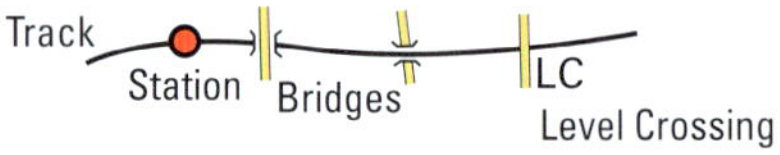

Track Station Bridges LC Level Crossing

Metro Rapid Transport System

Metro Station Bridges LC Level Crossing

P&R Park & Ride

Track

Tourist Information

- **P** Parking
- **i** Information centre, open all year
- *i* Information centre, seasonal
- Public toilet
- Cafe/tea-room
- Public house
- **H** Hospital
- Bike shop/repairs
- Bike shop/repairs Summer only
- Shop/Farm shop
- **V** Visitor centre
- Services
- Nature reserve
- Picnic site
- Walks/trails
- **BH** Bunk house
- Camp site/caravan site
- Viewpoint
- Public telephone
- Youth hostel
- Golf course
- Selected places of tourist interest

General Information

- Current or former place of worship with spire, minaret or dome
- Current or former place of worship with tower
- + Place of worship
- CH Club house
- PH Public house
- CG Cattle grid
- MP Mile post
- Mast
- Wind pump, wind turbine
- Buildings
- Glasshouse
- Electricity power line/pylons
- Marsh or salting
- Landfill site
- Trig point
- ·128 Heights to the nearest metre above mean sea level
- Crags/cliffs/outcrops
- Slopes
- **Danger Area** Firing, testing range/area. Danger! Observe warning notices
- Northumberland National Park boundary

General Information

- Coniferous woodland
- Mixed woodland
- Non-coniferous woodland
- Forestry Commission land
- National Trust - always open

Water Features

Footbridge, Bridge, Rocks, Shingle, sand, Mud, Lighthouse used, Ford, High water mark, Low water mark, Sand dunes

Archaeological

Archaeological sites non-Roman

- Cairn
- Fort
- Cup & Ring marked Rocks
- Battlefield (with date)
- + Site of antiquity
- Embankment/ditch
- ○ Monument

Archaeological sites Roman

MILECASTLE 29 (SITE OF)

7

The joys of cycling

Whether it's to boost your fitness, health or bank balance or as an environmental choice, taking up cycling could be one of the best decisions you ever make. Generally speaking, cyclists ride bikes for utility, recreational or sporting reasons, preferring to ride on-road or off-road routes.

This guidebook will help you enjoy cycling recreationally, whether on-road or off-road. It will point you to some of the best, easy or moderate cycle routes in Northumberland and Tyneside.

Terminology

On-road = 100% tarmac, entirely suitable for road bikes but hard work on a mountain bike

Off-road = on a mix of legal tracks and paths, sometimes linked by minor roads

Shared-use = usually level, traffic-free routes for cyclists, walkers and horse & riders

Grading

The routes in this guidebook comply with one of these three grades:

Easy = a route which is generally flat – suitable for less fit cyclists

Moderate = a route which has undulations – suitable for quite fit cyclists

Family-friendly = suitable for accompanied cycle-competent children aged 10+

There are no routes in this guidebook in the two following grades:

Difficult = a route suited to fitter, more skilled cyclists with reasonable stamina

Challenging = a demanding route that requires a high level of skill, fitness and stamina

Health benefits of cycling

"Cycling offers one of the most accessible and enjoyable ways to exercise, whether as part of a daily commute or a leisure pursuit. Cancer, diabetes, dementia, heart attacks and strokes are all decreased in those who exercise regularly. But it is not just an investment in one's future, for exercise offers much more immediate rewards, being an effective treatment for stress and low mood. It decreases rates of headaches and improves sleep, amongst other positive things. It has been said that if exercise were a drug, given the size of the benefits it would be the most heavily marketed and prescribed drug ever. As a life improving means which is free, I hope this excellent book encourages you to take to the wheels".

Dr Paul Goldsmith
MA BM BCh MRCP PhD

How to use this book

33 Cycle Routes in Northumberland & Tyneside has been designed to make it simple for you to **discover** some of the best leisurely cycle routes, graded easy to moderate and up to 30 miles in length.

The next step is to choose a route which you can get to and from that suits your bicycle, your cycling ability, fitness and available time.

Then it's time to prepare to cycle the route, which means checking:

- **your bike is roadworthy**
- **you have appropriate clothing and kit** – see the section on page 11
- **the weather forecast** – especially the wind-strength and direction
- **the location of Loos & Brews**
- **the details of nearby bike shops and bike taxis** – just in case!
- **the best way to get to and from the route**
- **can you cycle from home, or use public transport or a bike taxi** – the latter is ideal for groups
- **any sections or locations that will require extra care.**

Once the planning is done, all you have to do is enjoy riding the route of your choice!

The Cyclist's Code of Conduct

Obey the rules of the road
Always follow the Highway Code

- Be considerate to other road users at all times
- Be courteous
- Always pass people & animals considerately
- Give way to walkers and horse riders – always slow down when passing
- Ring your bike bell or politely call out to warn them of your approach
- Be especially considerate to other users on shared-use sections
- Thank people who give way to you.

Be countryside aware

- Follow the country code, particularly respecting wildlife, stock and crops
- Close all gates you pass through, unless found open. **Groups** – ensure the last person knows to close or leave open any gates
- Avoid erosion by braking carefully
- Take all litter home, including banana and orange peel
- Show goodwill to all engaged in rural industry – farm/forestry activities always take precedence
- Expect to meet cattle, sheep and horses and behave appropriately.

Look after yourself and others

- Make sure your bike is suitable and in good condition
- Take special care at junctions, when cycling downhill, and on loose surfaces
- Plan your route and cycle within your limits
- Wear a suitable cycle helmet correctly
- Wear conspicuous, weather-suitable clothing (for safety reasons)
- Carry water, food, repair items, route-map, waterproofs and spare clothing
- Carry money, personal ID and don't rely on mobile phone reception
- Avoid remote sections in bad weather
- Use lights when needed.

Meeting horse riders

- Expect to meet them at any time! NEVER pass quickly or closely
- Warn riders and horses of your approach by politely calling out
- Stop and back away from nervous horses, or if asked to do so by the rider
- Lay your bike flat if the horse is alarmed, until it is safe to continue
- Open/close gates for horse riders if sensible to do so
- REMEMBER: most horse riders live nearby and ride daily – you are probably just passing through.

Care of the environment

- Make every effort to travel to/from the route sustainably, i.e. on public transport, by car-sharing, taxi or bike
- Groups, individuals & users of support vehicles – please don't 'patrol' the route or block road sections or gateways. Switch off the engine when parked. It is insensitive to supply your group outside a tea-room or public house. Proprietors also appreciate it if you contact them before your visit
- Always ask to use a non-public toilet. Support your local café and tea-room and buy something
- Always check the forecast before setting off:
  www.metoffice.gov.uk or www.bbc.co.uk/weather/mobile
  for a free smart phone app
- Plan your journey.

BE SAFE! BE SEEN!

Don't be a cycling fashionista and wear black! Be seen! be safe!.

Safety and tips for a successful ride

Cycle helmets

This is your personal choice but this publication recommends you wear a helmet that's the right size for your head and is worn correctly. That means you can just fit two fingers under the chin strap and the front of the helmet sits just above, and parallel with, your eyebrows.

Clothing: kit and caboodle

Experienced cyclists will have learnt what to wear and take with them on a cycle ride but novice cyclists will find this summary helpful. Time of year, anticipated weather conditions and cycle group combination are key considerations.

Think carefully about the three points of contact you have with your bike every time you ride it, namely your feet, your bottom and your hands.

Your feet – wear comfortable shoes with firm soles and decent in-soles. This will allow you to press on each pedal through the ball of your foot without discomfort and allow you to walk comfortably if and when you need to.

Your bottom – to avoid chafing and bum pain, pay extra attention to this part of your anatomy! There's no need to wear lycra but it IS recommended you wear padded under-shorts at the very least – the thicker and better the quality, the more comfortable you will be. Wear ordinary baggy shorts or track-suit legs over them if you wish, but make sure the latter are close to your ankles to avoid being caught on the cogs of your front-chain wheel. Jeans are not recommended.

Your hands – except in cold weather, finger-less gloves with padded palms are the popular choice because they optimise finger dexterity and absorb bumpiness.

Eyewear – particularly important during the summer months when flying insects can be a nuisance.

Upper body – if it's a hot day, a breathable wicking T-shirt will be fine; that means it will wick away sweat and dry quickly if it gets wet for any reason. Cotton T-shirts just act as blotting paper! These can leave you feeling uncomfortable. A fleece makes a good outer layer and when needed, an outer wind - and - showerproof, single-skin top is recommended as it will do what it's supposed to do and fold up small when not being worn.

Hot days – use sun cream and top up regularly, particularly on your nose and the nape and sides of your neck; always wear sunglasses.

Cold days – still go cycling but remember nothing beats layering; be sure none of your layers are impermeable, otherwise first of all you will overheat and become sticky and then you will cool down and chill with unpleasant consequences.

Wet days – the best advice is give recreational cycling a miss if it's dank, mizzly or actually raining, but if you are caught out whilst on your bike then make sure your kit is good enough to keep you warm, reasonably dry and safe.
BE SEEN! BE SAFE!

You can cycle all year round if you wear the right clothing.

Panniers and rucksacks – it's lovely to cycle unencumbered so it's a good idea to minimise what you take with you but on the length of recreational rides this book promotes, it probably makes sense that at least one person carries a small rucksack – ideally, brightly-coloured with elastic-topped net side pockets that will carry a drink bottle or even two. Panniers can be a great addition to your bike if you intend to carry more on longer rides.

Useful items to take with you

A half-day recreational cycle ride isn't a major expedition but it pays to take the minimum of items with you just in case. This is a list of useful items you should consider taking with you to deal with minor events:

Bicycle pump with the correct valve fitting for your bike and others with you

Spare inner tube that fits your bike and others with you

Puncture kit – having practised how to use it!

Mobile phone with an ICE number for others to use IN CASE OF EMERGENCY

Money

An **Identity card** of some sort

Picnic (unless you have planned a café stop)

Spare energy food for yourself and for others

Small first aid kit – elastoplasts, antiseptic cream, antihistamine cream (for bites and stings), 4" crêpe bandage, 4 large safety pins; this will cover most minor skirmishes

Multi-tool – for minor adjustments

A handlebar map holder can be useful to keep you on the right track.

Travel and transporting your bike

When possible, cycle from your home or accommodation or use bike-carrying public transport (check before leaving home) **or book a bike taxi** (car or minibus with bike trailer depending on group size).

The directory below is not exhaustive as provision of this type is growing.

When using a bike taxi, when possible book it to take you to the start of your route so that you cycle back to your start point, base or home without pressure to meet transport at a certain time.

Public transport:
www.travelinenortheast.info – an easy way to plan your public transport
East Coast Railway (to book bike spaces) **www.eastcoast.co.uk**
Tyne Valley line (on a first arrived basis; 2 places on most – some carry 4)
email: **assistance@northernrail.org** – 08456 045 608

Bike taxis:
Amble: Pedal Power: www.pedal-power.co.uk 01665 713448

Berwick-upon-Tweed:
  A to B Taxis: 07732 520385 – 4, 6, 8 seats – can carry 2 bicycles
  A1 Cabs: 01289 331565 – can carry 2 bicycles
  Fife's Taxis: 01289 307188 – can carry bicycles with wheels removed
  Woody's Taxis: 07591 933233 – 3, 4, 6 and 8 seats – can carry bicycles

Wooler: Ron's Taxis 01668 281281

South East Northumberland: Watbus: www.watbus.org.uk – bike hire

Bellingham:
  Tarset Taxis: **ronnieingledew@btinternet.com** 01434 240835 / 077101400152
  www.milburnluxurycoaches.co.uk 01434 230 696 / 07777 663 210 – minibus & bike trailer

Hexham:
  Eco Cycle Adventures: **www.600600.co.uk/bike-transport**
  Hadrian's Wall Taxis: **www.hadrianswalltaxis.com**
  Advanced Taxis: **www.advancedtaxis.com**

Bike shops, cycle hire & repair services

Alnwick: www.thebikeshopalnwick.co.uk – 07599 350000
Amble: www.breezebikes.co.uk – 01665 710323
Berwick-upon-Tweed: Berwick Cycles: www.berwickcycles.co.uk – 01289 331476
Bedlington: Jim's Cycles – 01670 828464
Consett: www.bits4bikes.co.uk 01207 501188
Cramlington and Newcastle: www.cjperformancecycles.com – 01670 712536
Gateshead: Team Cycles, Team Valley: www.teamcycles.com – 0191 300 1590
Kirkley, near Ponteland: www.kirkleycycles.com – 01661 871094
Kielder Village: The Bike Place (shop, hire, repairs) www.thebikeplace.co.uk – 01434 220120
  Kielder Leaplish Waterside Park (summer only)
Morpeth: Sims Cycle Workshop: www.simscycleworkshop.com – 01670 504376
Newcastle: Edinburgh Cycle: www.edinburghbicycle.com – 0345 2570808
  Start Cycles: www.startfitness.co.uk/cycles-shop – 0191 6071364
  www.thecyclehub.org – 0191 276 7250
North Shields: Tyne Cycle (service and repairs) www.tynecycles.co.uk – 0191 259 2266
Prudhoe: www.giant-newcastle.co.uk – 01661 830618
Whitley Bay: Dixons Cycles: www.tynecycles.co.uk – 0191 253 2035
Wooler: Haugh Head: www.haughheadgarage.co.uk – 01668 281316

Other:

Pedal Power: www.pedal-power.co.uk – bike hire
Cycle Northumberland: www.cyclenorthumberland.org.uk –
  online portal for everything for cycling in Northumberland.
Eco Cycle Adventures: www.ecocycleadventures.co.uk – 01434 610076 Transport, hire including eBikes.
Stanley Taxis: www.stanley-travel.com – groups
The Bicycle Transport Company: www.thebicycletransportcompany.co.uk – Whickham – 01207 240400
www.newcastlecitytours.co.uk – 07780 958679 – bike hire

Accommodation

See www.visitnorthumberland.com/where-to-stay

At going to press all routes, facilities and information were correct but unforeseen circumstances may change in varying degrees.
Please kindly advise the publisher Northern Heritage of any changes using the contact details on page 2.

Road Routes
12 Easy to Moderate Routes

Cyclists on Route 11. Photo: © Andy McCandlish/www.andymccandlish.com

Road cycling

ROAD ROUTES

Northumberland is one of England's biggest counties, but it's also the least populated and the least visited which means that with the right map and guide, you can ride your bike all day and seldom see a soul.

Stretching between Tyne and Tweed, North Sea and Cheviot Hills, Northumberland is covered by a fine, capillary-like network of ancient winding country lanes linking isolated farms, tiny hamlets and villages. Quiet minor roads link these to sleepy market towns, where accommodation and good food is available in abundance.

Northumberland National Park extends from Hadrian's Wall in the south to the Cheviot Hills and Scottish Border in the north. Kielder boasts the biggest man-made forest in Europe and Kielder Water, the largest man-made lake in Europe. Kielder is a Mecca for off-road cyclists because it has countless tracks and man-made trails that are ideal for cycling.

Northumberland is one of the most rewarding counties to cycle in. Riding along its beautiful country lanes is a delightful experience. However, designing a series of cycle routes that take in all the scenic splendour while avoiding the few cycle-unfriendly highways, requires expert local knowledge and many years of cycling experience.

This book, compiled by one of the UK's most highly experienced cycle tourism specialists, offers a selection of 12 short to medium length routes on road, almost all entirely on tarmac. You can cycle any route in this book confident in the knowledge that it has been carefully constructed with safety, enjoyment and attractive scenery in mind.

The 12 selected road routes in this section combine a mix of country lanes, minor roads, cycle paths (usually adjacent to main roads), parts of the National Cycle Network and a few off-highway, hard-topped cycle paths, suitable for all types of bike. Bear in mind that while it's perfectly OK to ride a bike with knobbly tyres on metalled roads, pedalling will be hard work when compared to cycling on a road bike with narrow tyres, or riding a hybrid bike with wider, smooth tyres.

Some of the 12 routes are close to each other but because of Northumberland's varied terrain, every route is different. The only way to discover which route is your favourite is to ride them all!

Happy cycling.

Road 1

Approaching Clarewood

Wylam & Matfen Loop

DISTANCE: 46.2 km / 29 miles

GRADE: Moderate

START/END
Wylam
FREE PARKING: Wylam Country Park car park, Main Road, Wylam (behind the War Memorial)

Alternative START/END
Low Prudhoe
FREE PARKING:
Low Prudhoe, Tyne Riverside Country Park (south side of the river)

Ordnance Survey maps:
Explorer 316 – Newcastle-upon-Tyne
Landranger 88 – Newcastle-upon-Tyne

SUMMARY: *The Wylam & Matfen Loop* has much to recommend it in that it links the Tyne Valley with the Stamfordham / Matfen area so popular with cyclists, before returning to the Tyne Valley. The line it takes makes best use of downhill sections to access the scenic minor road adjacent to the River Tyne. The last section between Ovingham and Wylam is likely to carry a little more traffic.

Best cycled anticlockwise, this loop gently ascends out of the Tyne Valley from Wylam to cross the A69 safely and the Military Road soon after, before curving westward to Stamfordham, having joined the *Reivers Cycle Route* to Matfen (NCN Route 10). The loop now heads south to re-cross the Military Road and the A69 some 5 km later, where it joins *Hadrian's Cycleway* (NCN Route 72) by means of a swooping downhill section past Thornbrough Kiln. There's more downhill before the final scenic section along the banks of the River Tyne to Ovingham and thence to Wylam.

ROUTE NOTES:

① Take the quieter, slightly longer route from Wylam to the B6528.
② TAKE EXTRA CARE turning right off the B6528.
③ TAKE EXTRA CARE on the B6318, especially when turning right.
④ TAKE EXTRA CARE the B6530, especially when turning right.

LOOS & BREWS:
Wylam: choice of public houses and tea-room
Stamfordham: Swinburne Arms – www.swinburnearms.com – 01661 886015
Matfen: The Black Bull – www.theblackbullmatfen.co.uk – 01661 855395
Matfen Village Store and tea-room – 01661 886202
Ovingham: two public houses
Tyne Riverside Country Park – Low Prudhoe: café / WC

17

Approaching Eachwick

TAKE EXTRA CARE
turning right off the B6528

Take the quieter, slightly longer
route from Wylam to the B6528

Blind bends

START/END

Alternative START/END

③ TAKE EXTRA CARE on the B6318 and especially when turning right

Total distance	46.2 km loop
	47.0 km car park
Total ascent / descent	481 metres

Not many people know that . . . Fenwick to the west of Stamfordham means the farm (wick) by the fen – the same marsh or part thereof, once known as Maeth's Fen which gave Matfen its name.

19

TAKE EXTRA CARE when cycling along the B6530 and when turning right

The quiet road on the way to Thornbrough Kiln

20

Road 2

Morpeth & Whalton Loop

Mitford Castle

DISTANCE: 34 km / 21.25 miles   **GRADE:** Moderate

SUMMARY: This gently undulating route takes in relatively quiet roads to the south-west of Morpeth with the possibility of a shortcut via Shilvington. The shortcut shown uses about 800 m of straight section of the B6524; yet another route option from Shilvington to Twizell Cottage isn't shown. Whilst this route is bi-directional, it is probably best cycled anticlockwise.

Starting on the western outskirts of Morpeth, the route first heads to Mitford on the B6343 where it turns up a short hill past the pub before dropping down to cross the River Wansbeck on a lovely old sandstone bridge and then passes Mitford's picturesque church and ruined castle. The continuation west reverses Route 3 before it turns south to Whalton, Ogle and Kirkley which, is its farthest point. The return to Morpeth via Saltwick and Tranwell is straightforward road cycling. A much shorter enjoyable loop is possible from Mitford via Gubeon.

START/END
Morpeth: west end
FREE PARKING:
west end of Morpeth, lay-by at the bottom of the hill just before joining B6343

Alternative START/END
Thorneyford Farm, Kirkley
PARKING:
Kirkley Cycles & Tea-room
Thorneyford Farm:

Ordnance Survey maps:
Explorer 325 –
Morpeth & Blyth
Landranger 81 –
Alnwick & Morpeth

ROUTE NOTES

(1) The shortish sections along two B roads will carry more traffic than the rest of the route.

LOOS & BREWS:

Morpeth: wide choice of public houses, cafés, restaurants and shops / WC

Mitford: The Plough Inn – 01670 512587

Whalton: The Beresford Arms – 01670 775273 –
www.theberesfordarms.co.uk

Kirkley: Kirkley Cycles & Tea-room,
Thorneyford Farm – www.kirkleycycles.com – 01661 871094

Kirkley Hall: Orangery tea-room – www.kirkleyhall.co.uk/tea-room.aspx –
01670 841 235

Gubeon: Coffee Shop, Gubeon Golf. (B6524) – 01670 519090
Gubeon Farm tea-room – 07860 675319

21

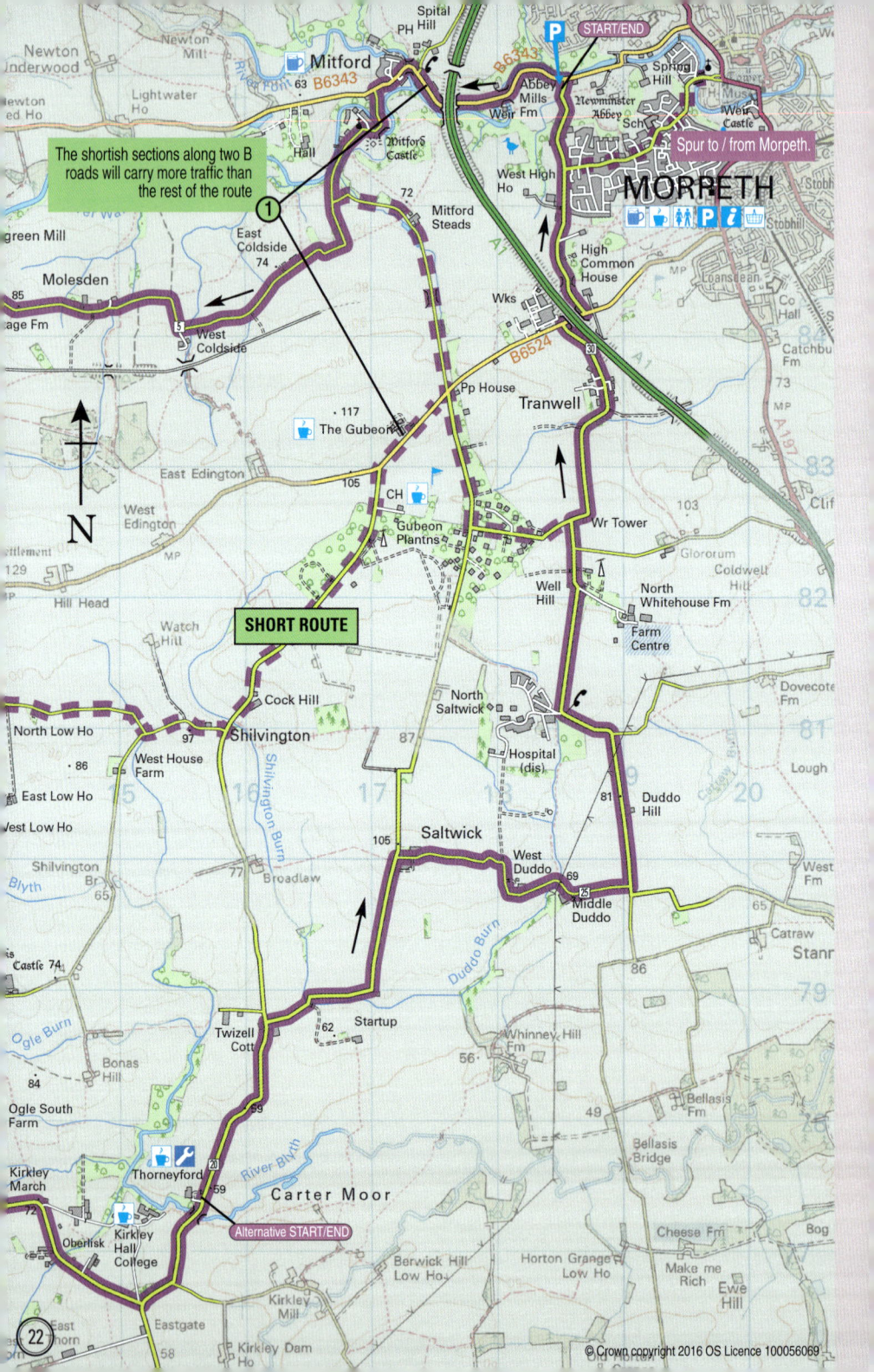

The shortish sections along two B roads will carry more traffic than the rest of the route

SHORT ROUTE

START/END

Spur to / from Morpeth.

MORPETH

Alternative START/END

Total distance	34 km
Total ascent / descent	327.6 metres

Not many people know that... Saltwick means the farm on the salt road, an old highway used to carry much needed salt made on the coast to out-by locations in Northumberland, as well as over the border into Scotland.

Not many people know that... the obelisk on 'a grassy knoll' near the southern tip of this route by Rev Newton Ogle (1726-1804), Dean of Winchester Cathedral, was placed there to commemorate the centenary of the landing in this country of William of Orange and his wife Mary and the 'Glorious Revolution' of 1688-9. The Ogles were the landed family who occupied Kirkley Hall nearby until 1922.

Road 3

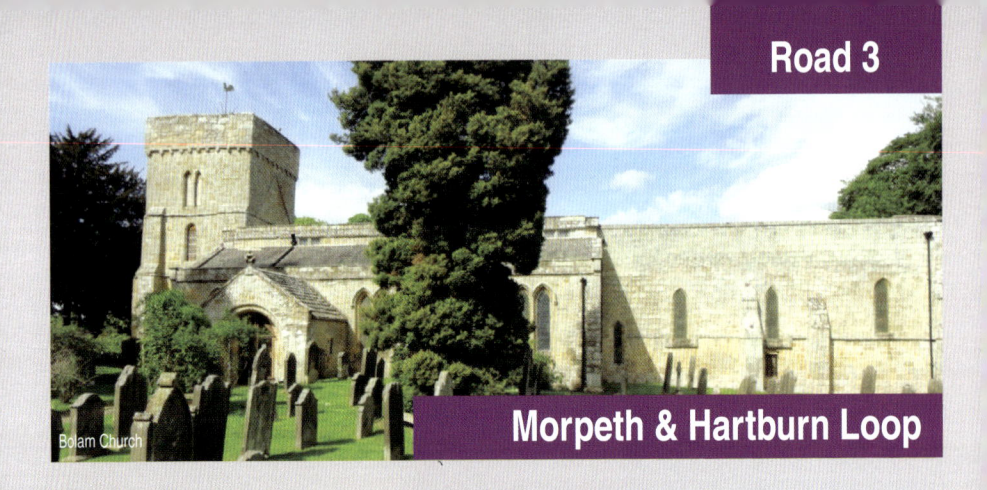

Morpeth & Hartburn Loop

Bolam Church

DISTANCE: 40 km / 25 miles

GRADE: Moderate

START/END
Morpeth: west end
FREE PARKING:
west end of Morpeth, lay-by at the bottom of the hill just before joining B6343

Alternative START/END
Hartburn
PARKING:
opposite the church

Bolam Lake Country Park
PARKING:
Bolam Lake Country Park

Ordnance Survey maps:
Explorer 325 – Morpeth & Blyth
Landranger 81 – Alnwick & Morpeth

SUMMARY: This longer bi-directional route is included in this guide, taking in a number of interesting hamlets to the west of Morpeth. It loops its way round the picturesque River Wansbeck, which is fed by several interesting streams and burns. This whole area has a rich history too varied to do more than hint at. Shallow river valleys mean inclines to descend and ascend which this route has aplenty, but in this case, all descents and ascents are short and picturesque – some extremely so.

Starting on the western outskirts of Morpeth, the route first heads to Mitford on the B6343. Here it turns up a short sharp hill towards Fair Hill, before turning generally north-west along a C road to follow the River Font, one of the Wansbeck's main tributaries. Turning almost due south, the route follows a quiet country lane to another C road, where the decision to complete the larger loop or take the shortcut must be made. The next section then threads together four very old churches at Hartburn, Bolam, Meldon and Mitford, each with its own history and unique charm. Albeit in ruins, Mitford Castle is a delight to cycle by, before the short ascent past the now unrecognisable Snuff Mill, (a former flannel manufacturing site), to Mitford. Then return to your starting point.

ROUTE NOTES

(1) No specific issues other than that the B6343 will carry more traffic than the rest of the route.

LOOS & BREWS:
Morpeth: wide choice of public houses, cafés, restaurants and shops / WC
Mitford: The Plough Inn – 01670 512587
Bolam Lake Country Park: café – 01661 881 234. WC
Dyke Neuk pub (shortcut): www.thedykeneuk.co.uk – 01670 772562

24

Cycling past Mitford Castle

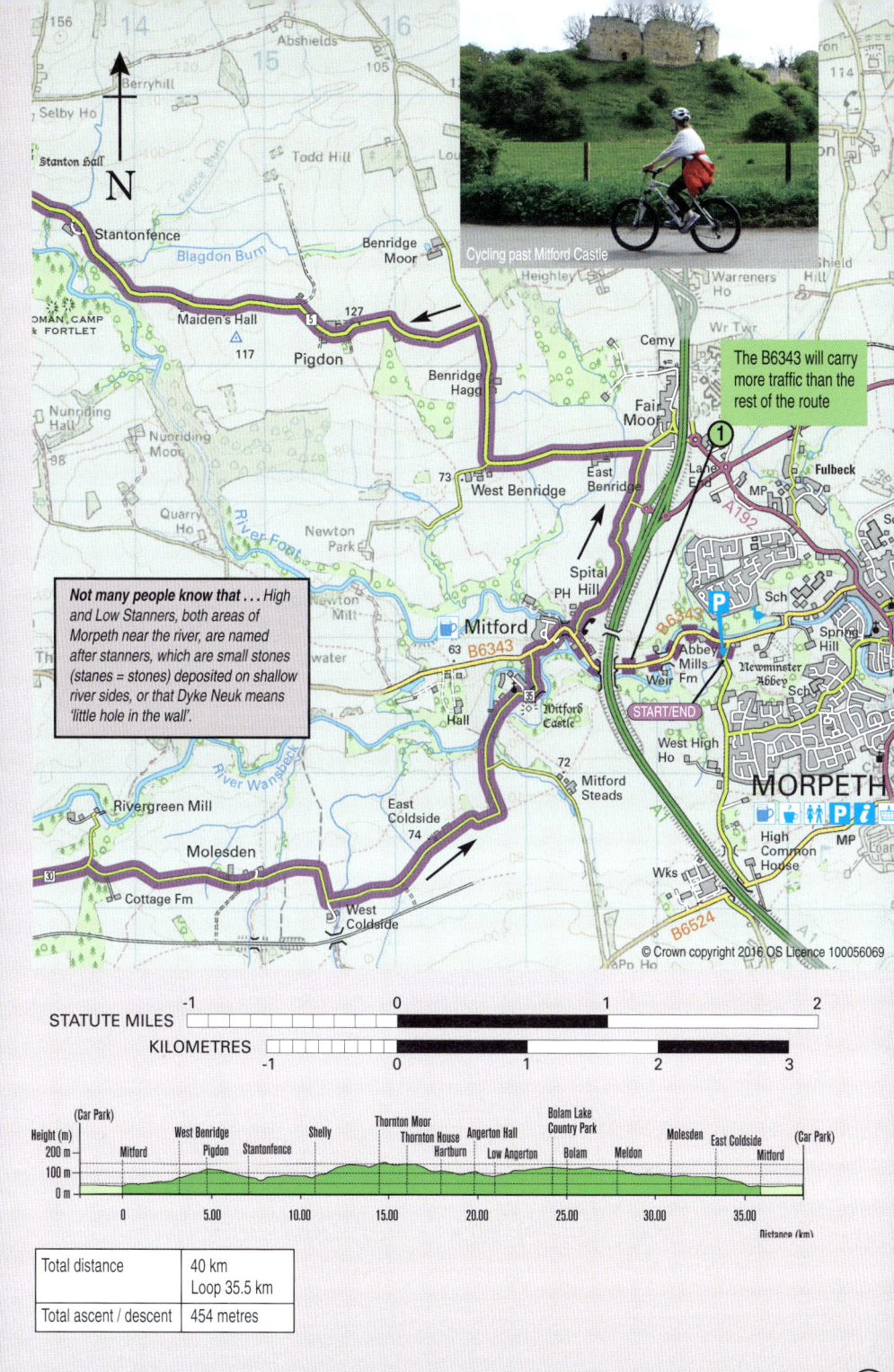

The B6343 will carry more traffic than the rest of the route

Not many people know that . . . *High and Low Stanners, both areas of Morpeth near the river, are named after stanners, which are small stones (stanes = stones) deposited on shallow river sides, or that Dyke Neuk means 'little hole in the wall'.*

Total distance	40 km
	Loop 35.5 km
Total ascent / descent	454 metres

25

The B6343 will carry more traffic than the rest of the route

①

SHORTCUT

Alternative START/END

Alternative START/END

Not many people know that . . . during WWII a German bomb was dropped on Bolam Church but it did not detonate, crashing through the church walls. The point of entry can still be seen today.

26

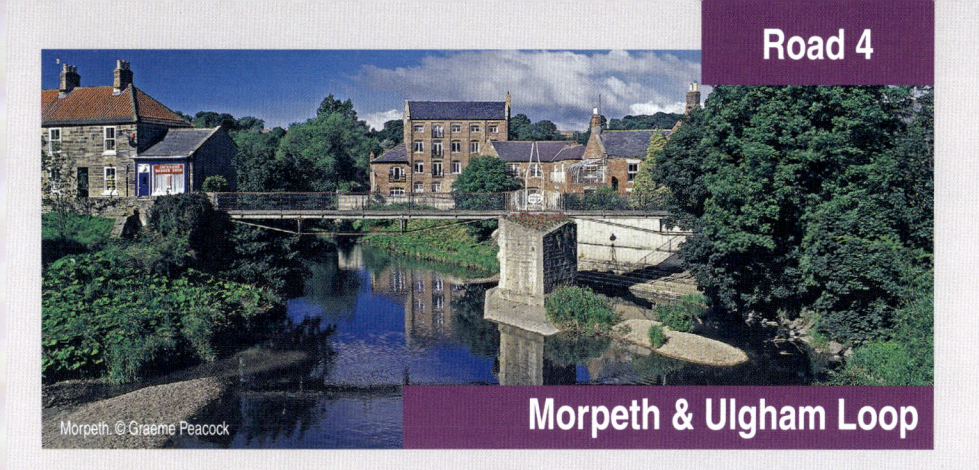

Road 4

Morpeth & Ulgham Loop

Morpeth. © Graeme Peacock

DISTANCE: 33.5 km / 21 miles

GRADE: Moderate

START/PARKING
Morpeth

PARKING: use the lay-by on the left of the A197, 250 m north of Morrison's supermarket

Family-friendly sections

Ordnance Survey maps:
Explorer 325 – Morpeth & Blyth
Landranger 81 – Alnwick & Morpeth

SUMMARY: This pleasant route to the north of Morpeth has been selected for inclusion in this guide book due to its location and the terrain it covers. It comprises quiet rural roads and also quite a long section of tarmac, off-highway verge path adjacent to the A167, which is signed NCN Route 155. The route is best cycled anticlockwise to get the A197 verge path out of the way early on, because the entry back into, and through, Morpeth is downhill and ridden with-flow. Starting on the north-east outskirts of Morpeth, a tarmac, off-highway verge path is easily followed for nearly 5 km until the quiet road link to Ulgham is reached, continuing on to Widdrington Station. Beyond this, Widdrington roundabout is accessed by 2 km of tarmac, off-highway verge path. The remainder of the route comprises quiet country lanes and rural C roads until the new Morpeth bypass is crossed after which Morpeth soon appears. Here the route stays in the left-hand lane until the left turn at the traffic lights and the town streets, which will return you to the starting point.

Not many people know that . . . going back centuries, the name Morpeth is a corruption of Murder Path, but there is no record of the original murder; whereas in the North of England and Scottish borders, a peth is a path on a hill.

ROUTE NOTES

(1) **TAKE EXTRA CARE** when crossing the A197 twice, once at the start of the route and then again at the roundabout crossing point after 1.5 km.

LOOS & BREWS:

Morpeth: Morrison's supermarket, choice of public houses, tea-rooms / WC

Ulgham: The Forge Inn – 01670 790793

Widdrington Station: shop, public house

Widdrington: The Widdrington Inn – www.thewiddringtoninn.co.uk – 01670 760260

27

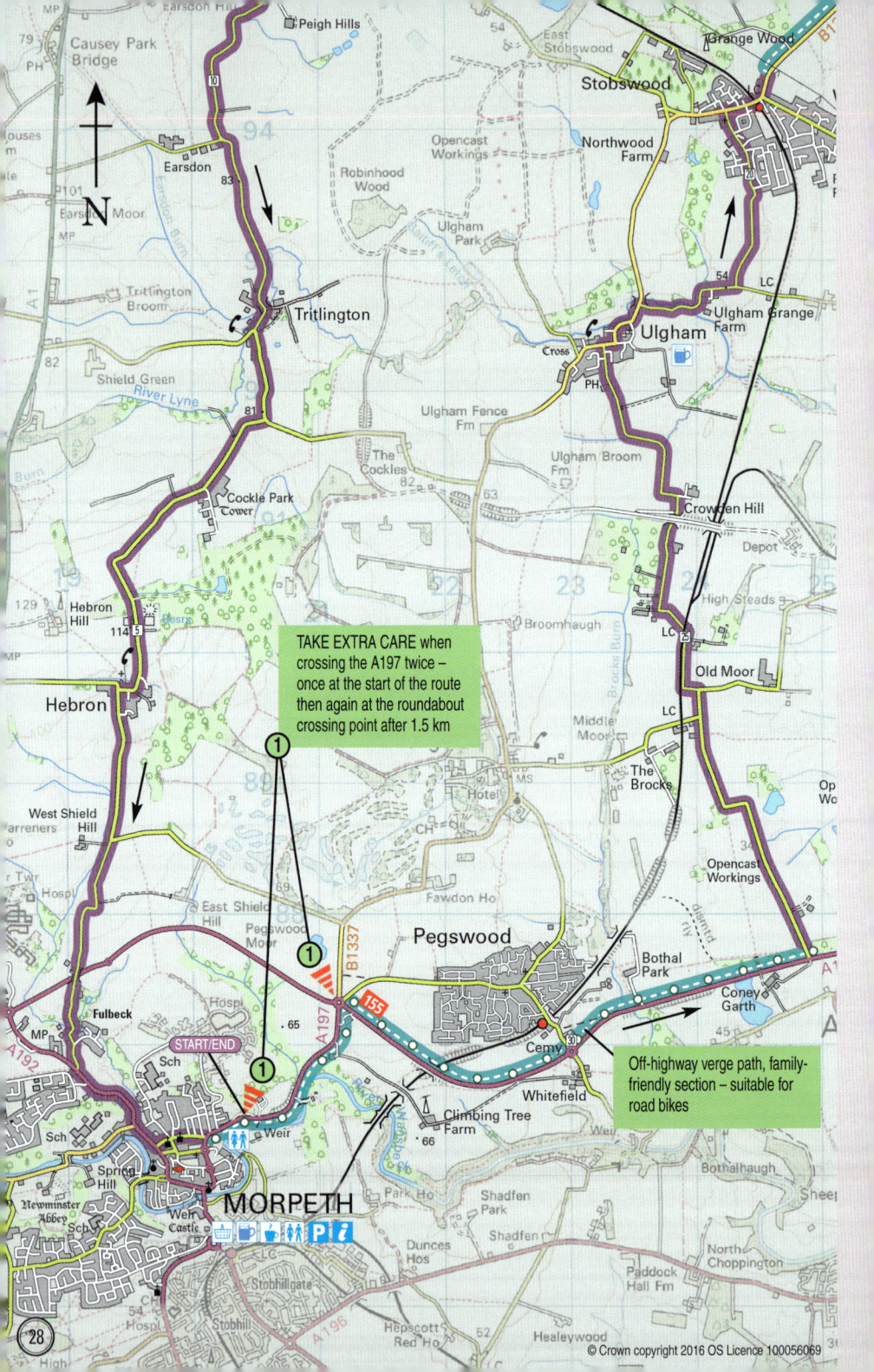

TAKE EXTRA CARE when crossing the A197 twice – once at the start of the route then again at the roundabout crossing point after 1.5 km

Off-highway verge path, family-friendly section – suitable for road bikes

© Crown copyright 2016 OS Licence 100056069

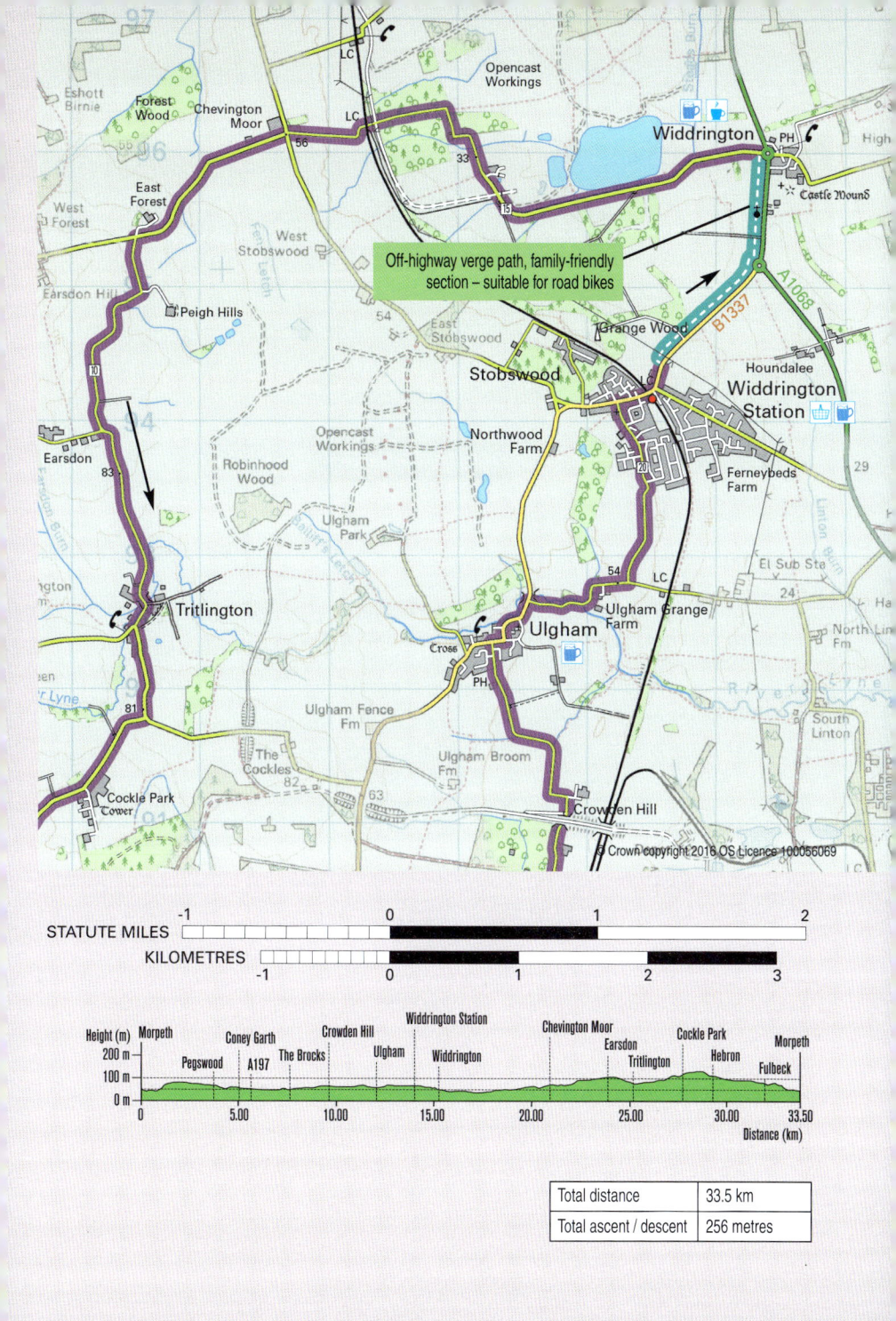

Off-highway verge path, family-friendly section – suitable for road bikes

© Crown copyright 2016 OS Licence 100055069

STATUTE MILES -1 0 1 2
KILOMETRES   -1 0 1 2 3

Height (m)
- Morpeth
- Pegswood
- Coney Garth / A197
- The Brocks
- Crowden Hill
- Ulgham
- Widdrington Station
- Widdrington
- Chevington Moor
- Earsdon / Tritlington
- Cockle Park
- Hebron
- Morpeth / Fulbeck

Distance (km)

Total distance	33.5 km
Total ascent / descent	256 metres

29

Road 5

Cresswell, Coast & Inland Loop

Queen Elizabeth II Country Park

DISTANCE: 29.4 km / 18.4 miles

Family-friendly sections

GRADE: Moderate

START/PARKING
Queen Elizabeth II Country Park
PARKING:
Queen Elizabeth II Country Park

INFORMATION:
www.visitnorthumberland.com/coast/druridge-bay

Ordnance Survey maps:
Explorer 325 – Morpeth & Blyth
Landranger 81 –
Alnwick & Morpeth

SUMMARY: This bi-directional route is an interesting mix of quiet roads, a section of the *Coast & Castles Cycle Route* (NCN Route 1) between Cresswell and Druridge and three significant sections of tarmac, off-highway verge path. There is a choice of cycling very pleasantly through Queen Elizabeth II Country Park past the lake, or around its outer perimeter but the latter bypasses toilets and refreshment. The outer perimeter option uses the tarmac, off-highway verge path which abuts the A197 and A189 although it is segregated from both.

Starting at the Queen Elizabeth II Country Park and ideally cycling anticlockwise, this easy road loop soon joins the *Coast & Castles Cycle Route* to head north along a tarmac verge path to the outskirts of Lynemouth where it rejoins the coast road for about 6 km / 3.6 miles. The route then cuts inland to Widdrington to use another section of tarmac verge path to Widdrington Station. Then on to Ulgham, where it turns south on mostly quiet rural roads to the A197, before heading east again along yet another section of tarmac verge path to link into Ashington. Blue cycle route signs for NCN Route 155 are followed optionally on a verge path, along High Market, then through several numerically named rows of houses until it's possible to cross the A197 for a short section of tarmac verge path to the entrance to Queen Elizabeth II Country Park and the hard top path past the lake to the start of this route.

Not many people know that . . . Ulgham is pronounced Uffam and derives its name from being haunted by owls.

LOOS & BREWS:
Queen Elizabeth II County Park: Woodhorn Grange – 01670 862332
Cresswell: shop – ice cream, snacks and drinks; public toilets.
The Drift Café – 01670 861599
Widdrington: The Widdrington Inn – www.thewiddringtoninn.co.uk – 01670 760260
Widdrington Station: shop, public house
Ulgham: The Forge Inn – 01670 790743

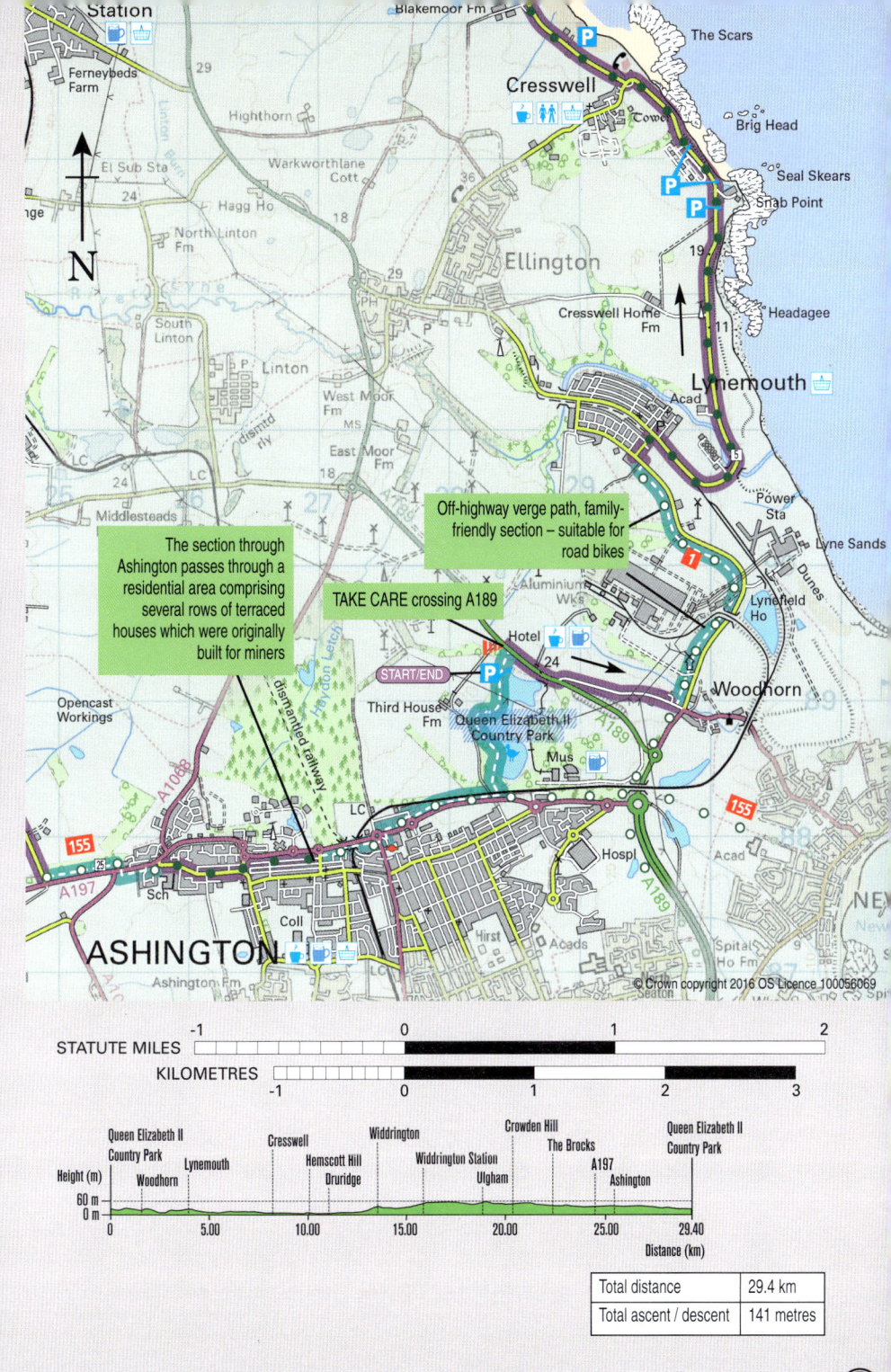

The section through Ashington passes through a residential area comprising several rows of terraced houses which were originally built for miners

Off-highway verge path, family-friendly section – suitable for road bikes

TAKE CARE crossing A189

START/END

Total distance	29.4 km
Total ascent / descent	141 metres

31

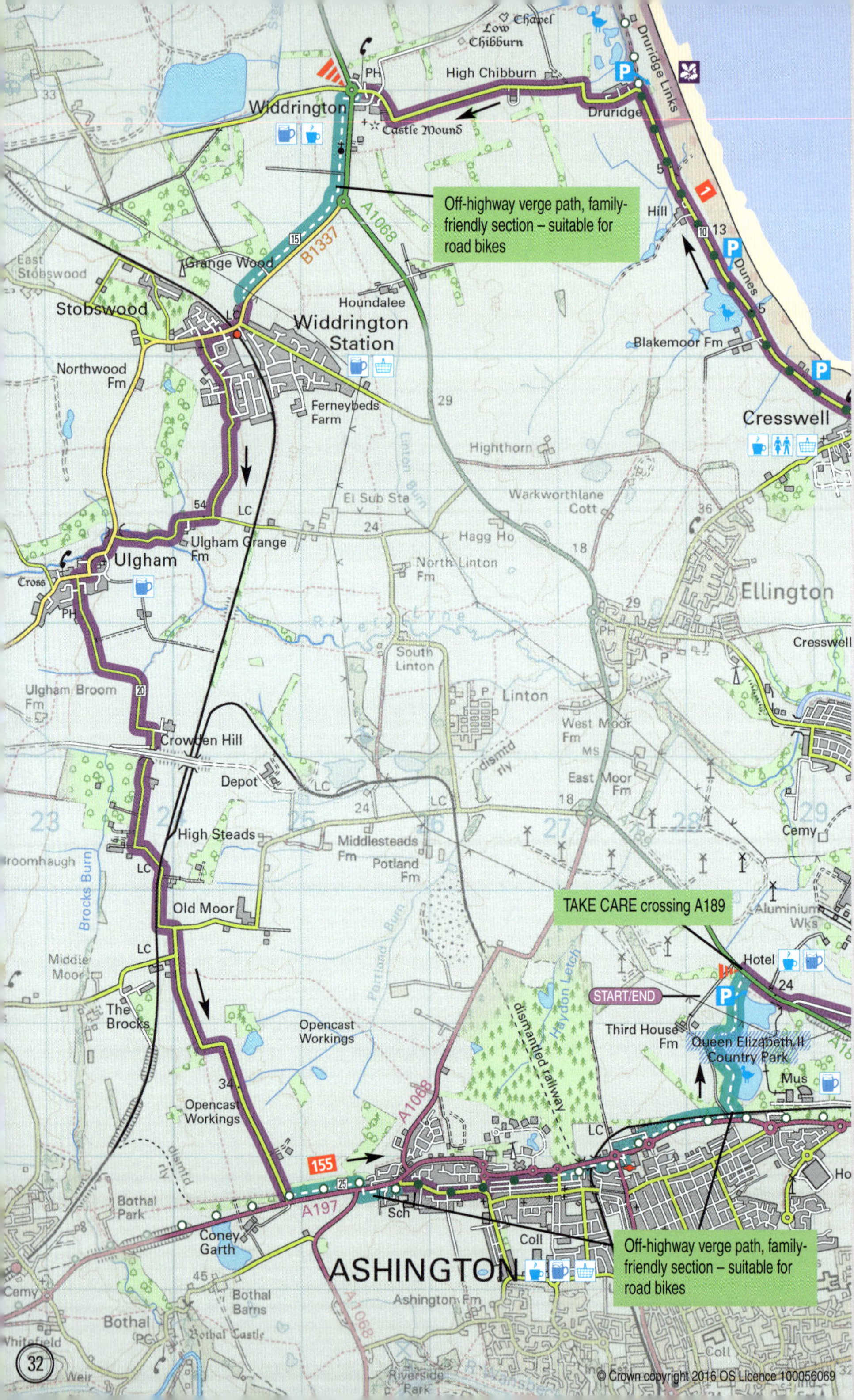
Low Chibburn
Chapel
Druridge Links
High Chibburn
Widdrington
Castle Mound
Druridge
Off-highway verge path, family-friendly section – suitable for road bikes
B1337
A1068
Grange Wood
East Stobswood
Stobswood
Houndalee
Widdrington Station
Hill
Dunes
Blakemoor Fm
Northwood Fm
Ferneybeds Farm
Cresswell
Highthorn
Linton Burn
El Sub Sta
Warkworthlane Cott
Ulgham Grange Fm
Hagg Ho
North Linton Fm
Ulgham
Cross
Ellington
River Lyne
South Linton
Cresswell
Ulgham Broom Fm
Linton
West Moor Fm
Crowden Hill
dismtd rly
Depot
East Moor Fm
High Steads
Middlesteads Fm
Potland Fm
A189
Cemy
Broomhaugh
Brocks Burn
TAKE CARE crossing A189
Aluminium Wks
Old Moor
Portland Burn
Hotel
Middle Moor
START/END
The Brocks
Opencast Workings
dismantled railway
Haydon Letch
Third House Fm
Queen Elizabeth II Country Park
Mus
Opencast Workings
155
A197
Sch
Bothal Park
Coney Garth
Coll
ASHINGTON
Off-highway verge path, family-friendly section – suitable for road bikes
Ashington Fm
Bothal Barns
Bothal
Bothal Castle
Whitefield
Weir
Riverside Park
Coll
Ho

Road 6

Warkworth & Shilbottle Loop

Warkworth from the air. © Graeme Peacock

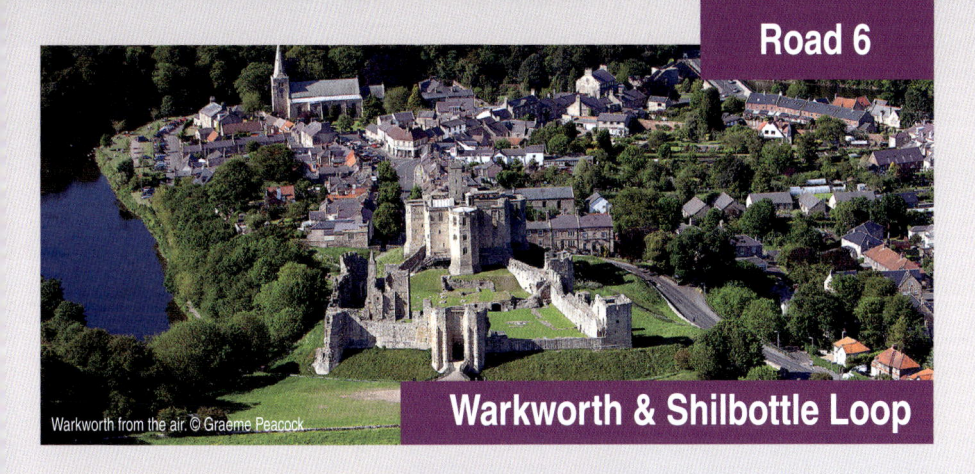

DISTANCE: 24.75 km / 15.5 miles

GRADE: Moderate

Family-friendly section

SUMMARY: Largely quiet roads with the last section off-highway; the A1068 is crossed once and ridden favourably for two short sections. Cycle clockwise to descend to the coast and enter Warkworth from the north with the traffic flow for the red section; there's a VERY narrow road approaching Hazon High Houses which may have grass in the middle and a few potholes.

This easy loop heads inland from Warkworth on its way to the very pleasant country lanes around the spread-out hamlet of Guyzance. Having first crossed the River Coquet by means of a footbridge, you should push your bike a short distance along the unsurfaced footpath adjacent to the river, to rejoin the road. After Guyzance the route gently ascends to Shilbottle and then descends from High Buston to cross the A1068 at right angles with good visibility. From there the route follows the shared-use, traffic-free *Coast & Castles Cycle Route* (NCN Route 1) to join the main road for the last section into Warkworth. The route can be shortened by bypassing Guyzance and then cycling via South Moor and Low Buston to rejoin the main route west of High Buston. Cycling to Alnmouth is an optional add-on.

LOOS & BREWS:
Warkworth: choice of public houses, cafés, restaurants and shops / WC at car park

Shilbottle: limited refreshments available (shop, public house and fish-and-chips)

> *Not a lot of people know that . . .* Guyzance originates from the linguistic corruption of the name Gysnes, a Norman who dedicated a chapel to St Wilfred de Gysnes at nearby Brainshaugh. Hardly a startling fact in itself, yet to this day Guyzance is so named.

START/END
Warkworth (Birling Car Park)

PARKING:
FREE: new Town Car Park, Warkworth

FREE: Warkworth Dunes Picnic Site: car park and picnic site / WC

Warkworth Castle Car Park: small charge to all visitors (including members) refunded upon admission to the castle

Ordnance Survey maps:

Explorer 332 – Alnwick & Amble

Explorer 340 – Holy Island & Bamburgh

Landranger 81 – Alnwick & Morpeth

Landranger 75 – Berwick-upon-Tweed

33

Cross the A1068 WITH CARE

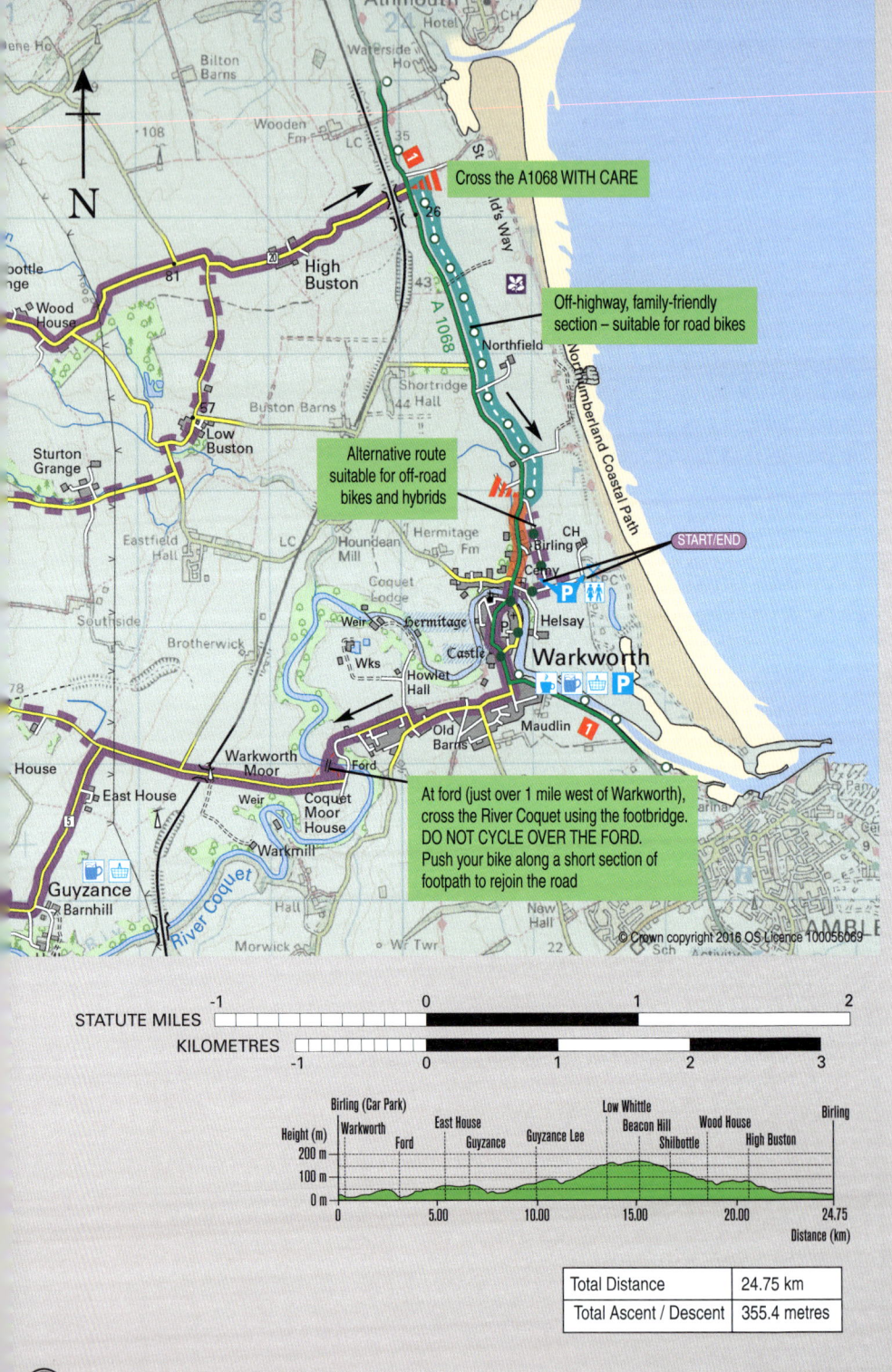

Off-highway, family-friendly section – suitable for road bikes

Alternative route suitable for off-road bikes and hybrids

START/END

At ford (just over 1 mile west of Warkworth), cross the River Coquet using the footbridge. **DO NOT CYCLE OVER THE FORD.** Push your bike along a short section of footpath to rejoin the road

Total Distance	24.75 km
Total Ascent / Descent	355.4 metres

34

Shilbottle
Middle Cawledge Park
West Cawledge Park
Black Plantn
Deanmoor
Colliery Fm
Townfoot
Longdyke
Dene Ho
Bilton Barns
Wooden Fm
Tyelaw Burn
Shilbottle Grange
Wood House
High Buston
South East Fm
Hillhead
Beacon Hill
Hitchcroft
Selby's Stead
Buston Barns
Low Buston
Sturton Grange
Grange Burn
Hampeth
Low Whittle
Whittle Colliery (dis)
South Moor
SHORTCUT
Hound Mill
Southside
Brotherwick
Hart Law
Newton Low Hall
Narrow road with poor surface in parts
Hazon High Houses
Bank House
Warkworth Moor
Ford
dismantled railway
Villa Fm
East House
Coquet Moor House
Warkmill
Hazon
Hazon Burn
Hazon Lea
Guyzance
Barnhill
Guyzance Lee
Hall
River Coquet
Morwick
Moor Ho
Brainshaugh
Whirleyshaws
Priory
Acton Dene
Mere Burn
Weir
Acton Ho
Cavil Head
Lane Head Fm
Acton
Acklington Park
© Crown copyright 2016 OS Licence 100056069

Road 7

Warkworth & Alnmouth Loop

Alnmouth

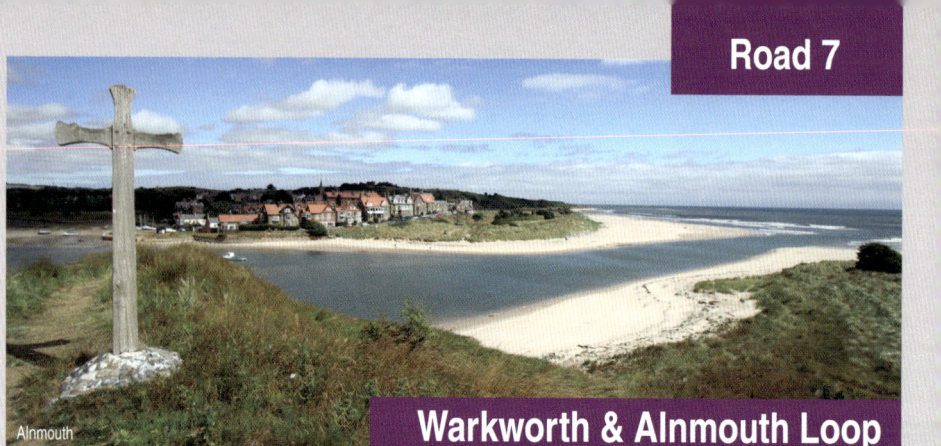

DISTANCE: 14.25 km / 9 miles

GRADE: Easy

START/END
Warkworth village

Family-friendly section

PARKING:
FREE: New Town car park, Warkworth

SUMMARY: This relatively short route is best done clockwise. It's included because it's a reasonably easy loop route between two iconic villages on the beautiful Northumberland coastline, mainly using minor, less busy roads. The inland section gently gains height in advance of the downhill through the hamlet of Bilton and over the mainline railway to the Hipsburn roundabout, where the A1068 is crossed. Alnmouth can either be accessed along the B1338, or the route started from there. The southbound leg uses the hard-topped, field edge path that leaves the B1338, then soon parallels the A1068 which isn't a cycle-friendly road. The last section into Warkworth is with-flow traffic, before returning to the start point.

Warkworth Dunes Picnic Site:
car park and picnic site / WC

Warkworth Castle car park:
Small charge to all visitors (including members) refunded upon admission to the castle

Alternative START/END
Alnmouth
PARKING: village car park – turn left after entering the main street; can be busy on summer days!

Ordnance Survey maps:
Explorer 332 – Alnwick & Amble
Landranger 81 – Alnwick & Morpeth

ROUTE NOTES:

① **TAKE EXTRA CARE** crossing Hipsburn roundabout. The B1338 carries greater traffic flow.

② Family-friendly section; suitable for road bikes.

LOOS & BREWS:
Warkworth: choice of public houses, cafés, restaurants and shops / WC
Alnmouth: public houses, restaurants, two tea-rooms, shops / WC

Not many know that ... at Christmas 1806, a huge storm changed the course of the river and this spelt the end for the once busy harbour. From this time Alnmouth declined in importance and gradually became the quiet village it is today. The river burst through the dunes once connected to the village, leaving a small cross separated from the village by the river.

TAKE EXTRA CARE crossing Hipsburn roundabout. The B1338 carries greater traffic flow

Spur to / from Alnmouth.

Alternative START/END

Off-highway family-friendly section – suitable for road bikes

START/END

Total distance	14.25 km
Total ascent / descent	188 metres

37

Road 8

Dunstanburgh Castle from the south. © Graeme Peacock

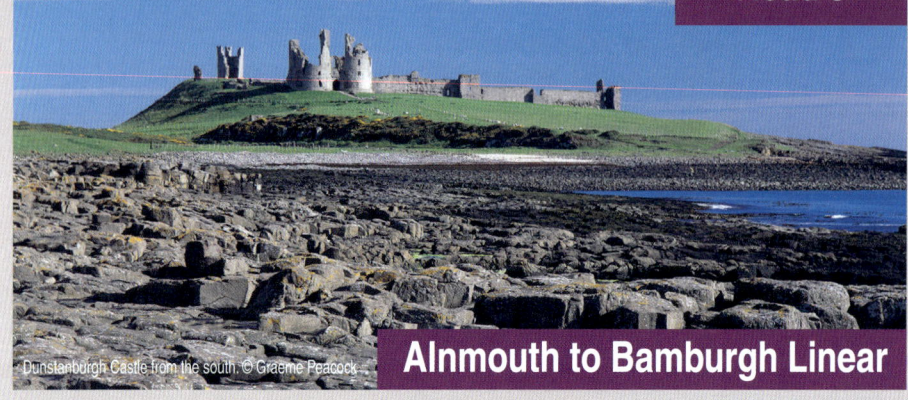

Alnmouth to Bamburgh Linear

DISTANCE: 43.6 km / 27.25 miles **GRADE:** Easy

SUMMARY: This linear route follows one of the most enjoyable sections of the *Coast & Castles Cycle Route* (NCN Route 1). The reason it goes inland via Chathill is because the B1339 between Embleton and Beadnell isn't deemed appropriate for the standard of routes this guide recommends, the same reason it wasn't used for the *Coast & Castles Cycle Route*. Navigation is straightforward – just follow the blue NCN Route 1 signs located at every junction.

OVERVIEW: This is a popular section of the *Coast & Castles Cycle Route* and you will see why when you cycle it. It calls in or passes through a number of memorable places and offers longer views of others. Alnmouth, Boulmer, Howick, Craster, Embleton, Seahouses and Bamburgh are the main call-in / pass-through places, whilst Dunstanburgh and the Farne Islands are the two outstanding views.

ROUTE NOTES

① Sections of the B road into and just after Longhoughton can be busy.

LOOS & BREWS:

Alnmouth: choice of public houses, restaurants, two tea-rooms, shops / WC
Boulmer: The Fishing Boat Inn – www.thefishingboatinn.co.uk – 01665 577750
Longhoughton: public house and village shop
Craster: Shoreline Café – 01665 571251; Pipers Pitch (van);
The Jolly Fisherman / WC – www.thejollyfishermancraster.co.uk – 01665 576461
Dunstan: The Cottage Inn – www.cottageinnhotel.co.uk – 01665 576658
(Ellingham): packhorseinn-ellingham.co.uk – 01665 589 2429
Embleton: Dunstanburgh Castle Hotel – www.dunstanburghhotel.co.uk – 01665 576111; shop / WC
Christon Bank: The Blink Bonny – 01665 576595
Seahouses: wide choice of public houses, restaurants and cafés / WC
www.visitnorthumberland.com/seahouses
Bamburgh: wide choice of cafés, public houses and restaurants / WC

START/PARKING
Alnmouth
PARKING: village car park – turn left after entering the main street; can be busy on summer days!

END: Bamburgh

Ordnance Survey maps:
Explorer 340 – Holy Island & Bamburgh
Explorer 332 – Alnwick & Amble
Landranger 75 – Berwick-upon-Tweed
Landranger 81 – Alnwick & Morpeth

Not many people know that ... a snook is a point, so Snook Point a little north of the very attractive hamlet of Low Newton-by-the-Sea really means Point Point.

38

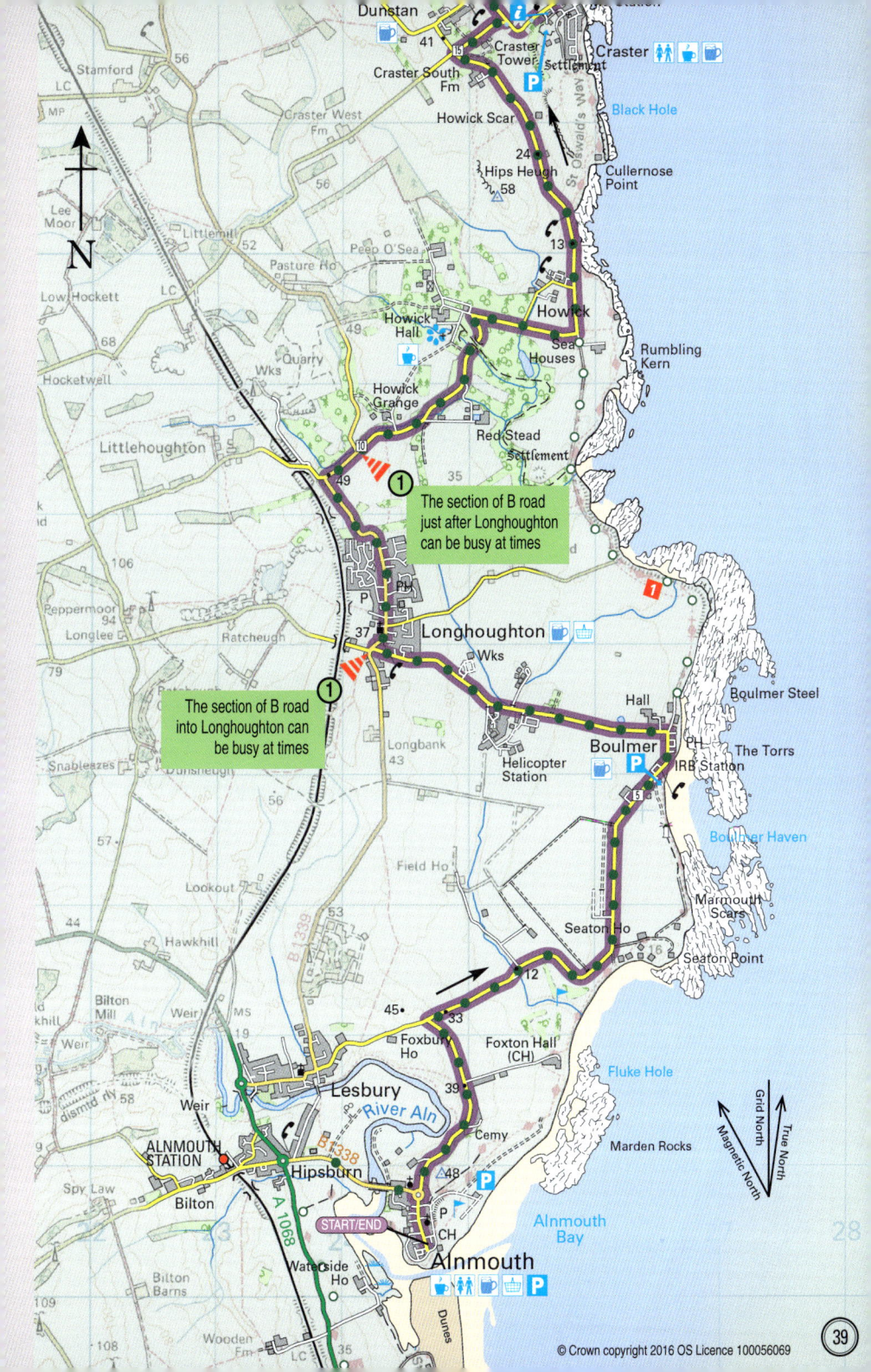

The section of B road just after Longhoughton can be busy at times

The section of B road into Longhoughton can be busy at times

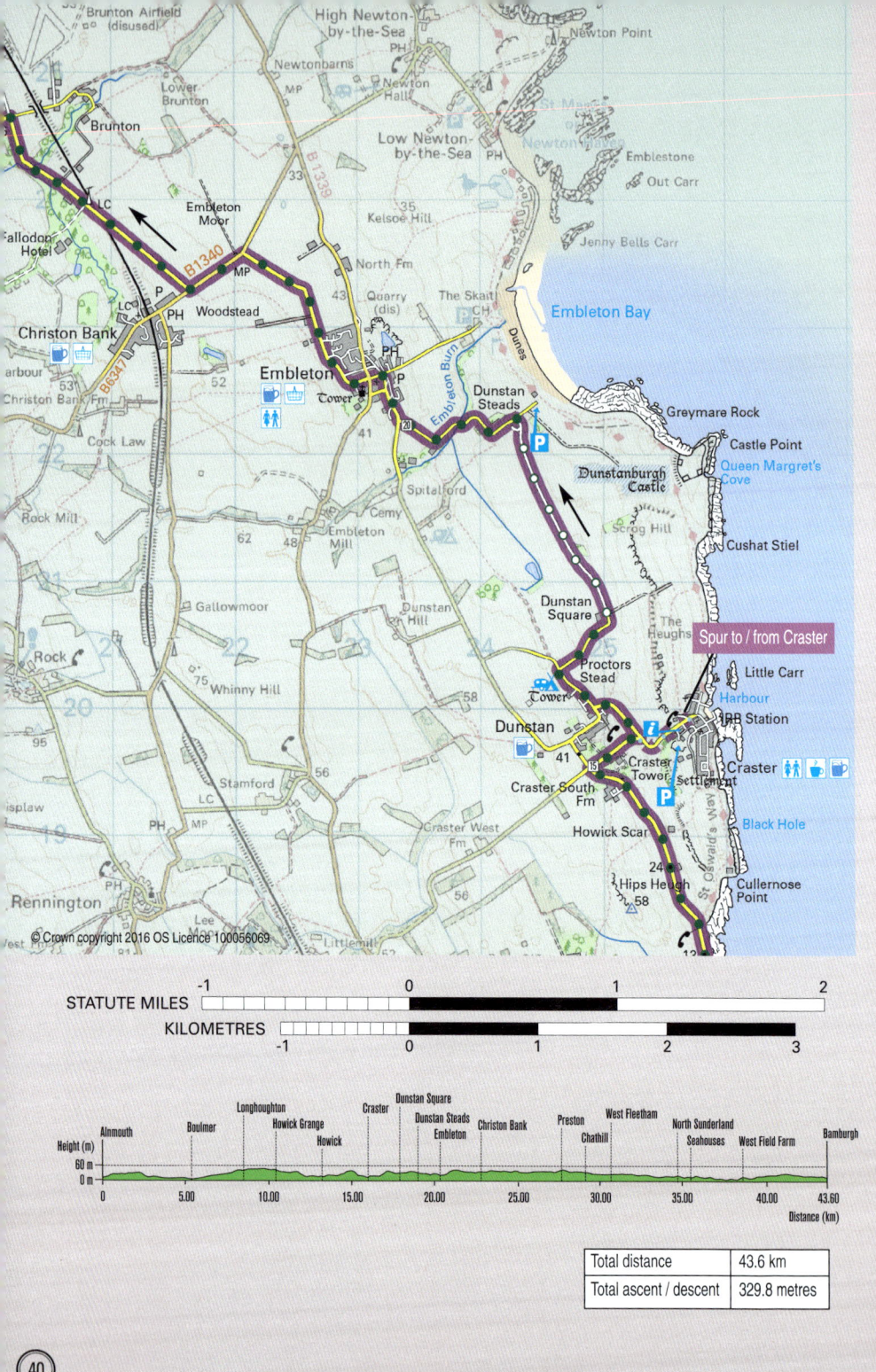

Total distance	43.6 km
Total ascent / descent	329.8 metres

40

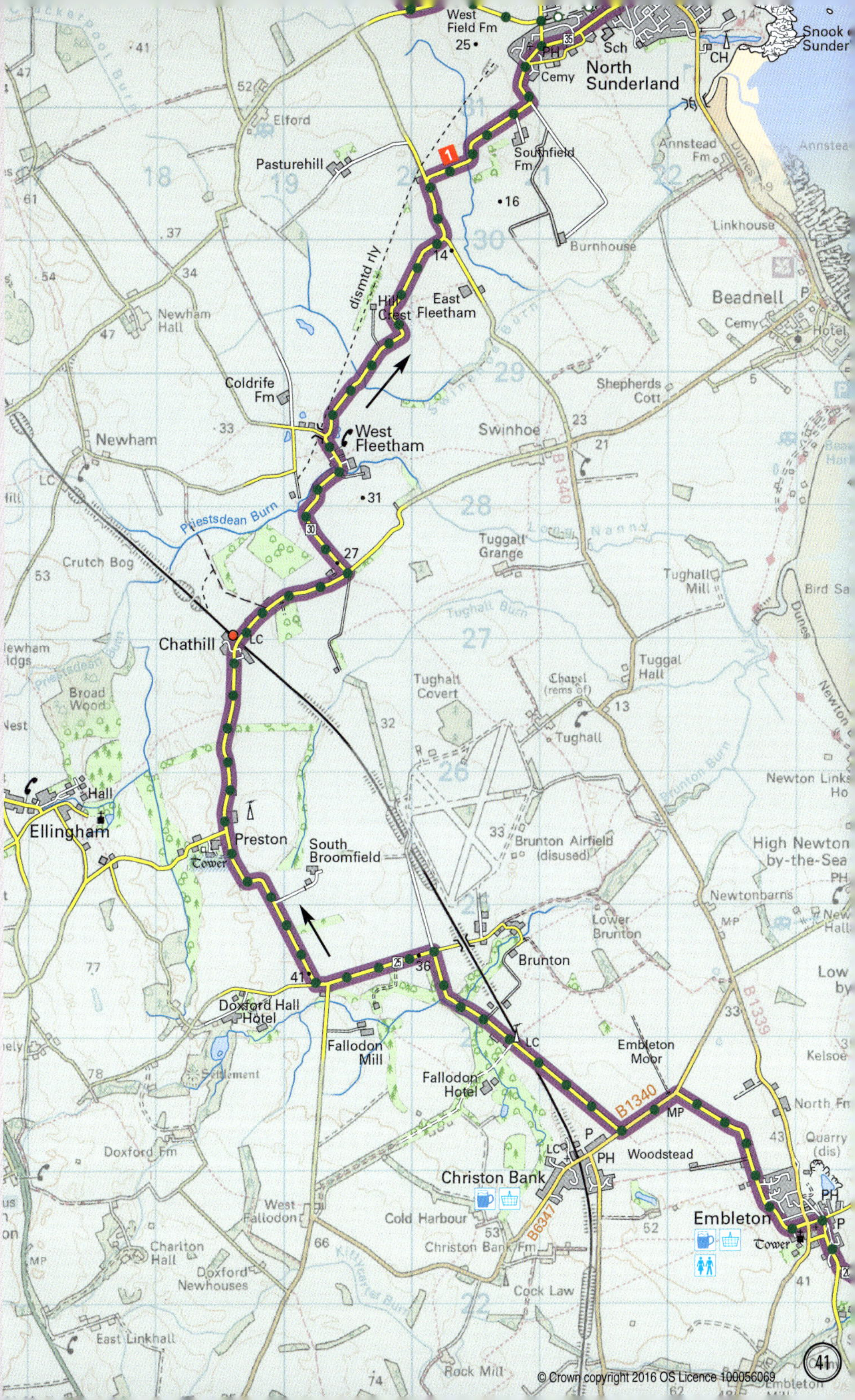

West Field Fm
North Sunderland
Sch
Cemy
PH
CH
Snook
Sunder
Elford
Pasturehill
Southfield Fm
Annstead Fm
Dunes
Burnhouse
Linkhouse
dismtd rly
Hill Crest
East Fleetham
Beadnell
Cemy
Hotel
Newham Hall
Coldrife Fm
Shepherds Cott
West Fleetham
Swinhoe
Newham
LC
Priestsdean Burn
B1340
Long Nanny
Tuggall Grange
Crutch Bog
Tughall Mill
Bird Sa
Chathill
Tughall Burn
Priestsdean Burn
Broad Wood
Tughall Covert
Chapel (rems of)
Tuggal Hall
Tughall
Newton
Brunton Burn
Newton Links Ho
Hall
Ellingham
Preston
Tower
South Broomfield
Brunton Airfield (disused)
High Newton by-the-Sea
PH
Newtonbarns
Lower Brunton
Brunton
Doxford Hall Hotel
Fallodon Mill
Embleton Moor
B1339
Kelsoe
Settlement
Fallodon Hotel
B1340
MP
North Fm
Quarry (dis)
Doxford Fm
PH
Woodstead
Christon Bank
Embleton
West Fallodon
Cold Harbour
B6347
Christon Bank Fm
Tower
Charlton Hall
Doxford Newhouses
Kittycarter Burn
Cock Law
East Linkhall
Rock Mill

Craster. Photo: © Graeme Peacock.

Grace Darling's Tomb, Bamburgh.
Photo: © Graeme Peacock

42

Road 9

Great views of the Cheviots from near Chatton

Belford, Chatton & Lowick Loop

DISTANCE: 41 km / 25.6 miles **GRADE: Moderate**

START/PARKING
Belford
FREE PARKING: on the B6349, a little to the west of the village

Ordnance Survey maps:
Explorer 340 –
Holy Island & Bamburgh
Landranger 75 –
Berwick-upon-Tweed

SUMMARY: This route is best cycled clockwise to take full advantage of the gradient. Essentially, it is the road cycle tour of the Kyloe Hills and the Sandstone Ridge, with views of the coast on the eastward side and views of the Cheviots on the western flank. Though not marked, it is possible to shorten the route by staying on the B6349 – the upward incline is soon over – and rejoining the route at West Lyam crossroads or even turning right at the top of the hill. Another shortcut option is to miss out Beal by turning right at Kentstone to join the B6353 into Fenwick. Both shortcuts will reduce the route by 8 km / 5 miles.

The Belford, Chatton and Lowick road loop ascends the Sandstone Ridge at its southern end and then drops down to Chatton. The inland northern spine up to Lowick is straight, being an old Roman road. It's also relatively flat as is the next section of the route to Beal. After this the route takes on an undulating quality all the way to Belford, where it ends with a nice downhill into the village.

> *Not many people know that . . .*
> *Detchant is a corruption of the word 'ditching', which probably goes back to far-off days when ditches were dug as boundaries. It's even thought the Scottish border extended this far south at one point in time and it's interesting to note that a little to the north of Detchant is the County Burn.*

ROUTE NOTES

① The downhills on the west side of the Sandstone Ridge need respect.

② **TAKE EXTRA CARE** crossing the A1 at Beal, or push your bike down the verge to avoid having to cross it.

LOOS & BREWS:

Belford: Bluebell Inn – 01668 213543; Sunnyhills Farm Shop tea-room – 01668 219662; village store, WC

Chatton: Lord Percy Arms – www.percyarmschatton.co.uk – 01668 215244; Post Office & village store

Lowick: The White Swan Inn – www.thewhiteswanlowick.co.uk – 01289 388248; village store

Beal: The Lindisfarne Inn – www.lindisfarneinn.co.uk – 01289 381 223; shop in garage 'Bike Station' tools

43

SHORT ROUTE

The downhills on the west side of the Sandstone Ridge need respect

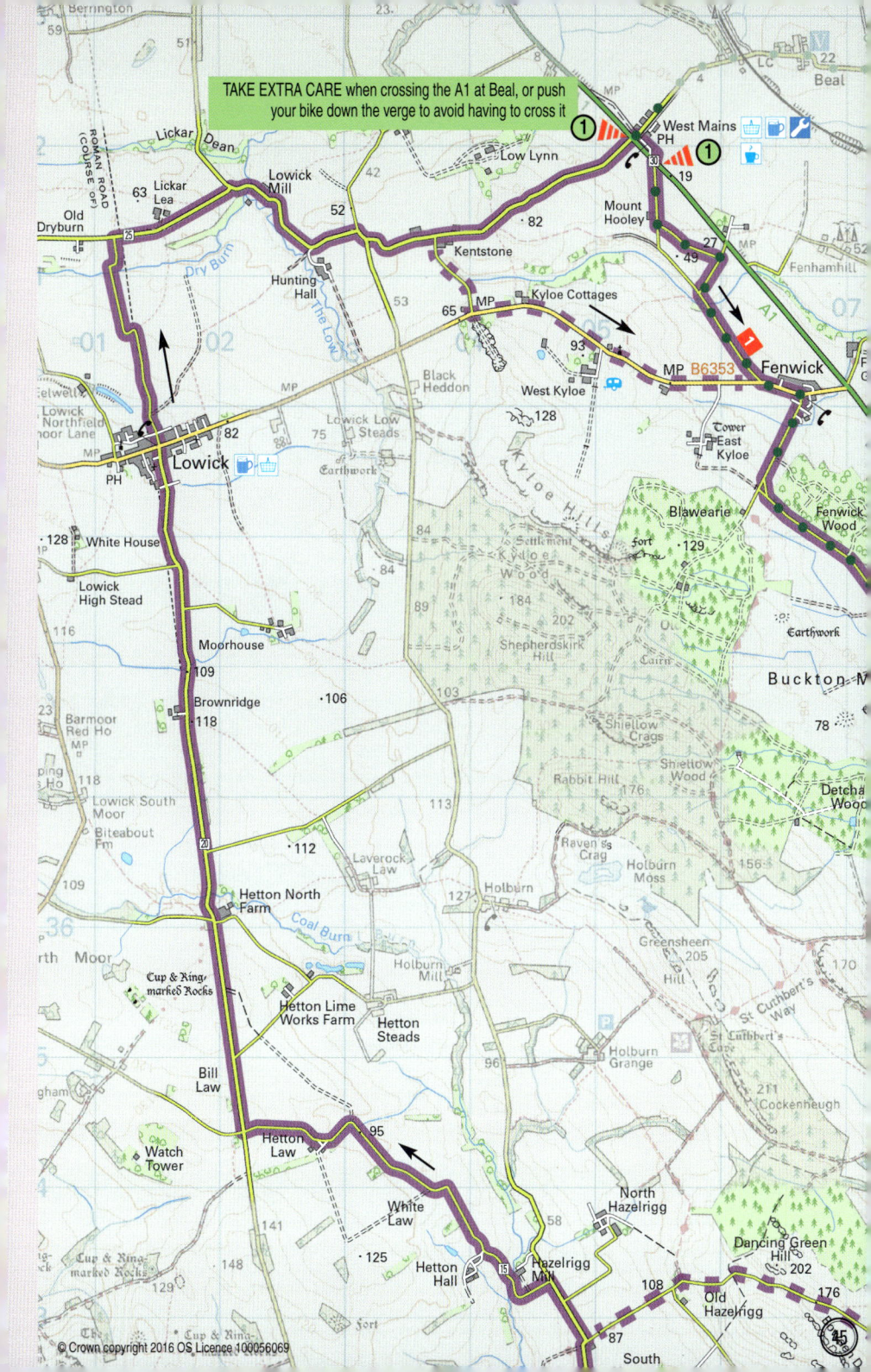

TAKE EXTRA CARE when crossing the A1 at Beal, or push your bike down the verge to avoid having to cross it

Total distance	41.00 km
Total ascent / descent	558 metres

Road 10

Bamburgh Castle

Seahouses, Bamburgh & Lucker Loop

DISTANCE: loop 29 km / 18 miles   **GRADE: Easy**

SUMMARY: This gently undulating, bi-directional route almost exclusively follows minor roads except for 2 km on the B1341 which coincide with the *Coast & Castles Cycle Route* (NCN Route 1). It also shares this signed cycle route between the hamlet of Preston and Seahouses. The only reason it avoids the coast road between Seahouses and Bamburgh is traffic volume during the main tourist season.

This easy inland loop links Seahouses with Bamburgh, gaining just enough height to provide views of the sea. Bamburgh Castle is a stunning sight, whether approaching the village from the south-east or the south-west. The minor roads which provide the spine of the route via Lucker are usually less busy, although the section between the hamlet of Preston and Seahouses carries more traffic.

LOOS & BREWS:
Seahouses: wide choice of public houses, cafés and restaurants / WC
Bamburgh: wide choice of public houses, cafés and restaurants / WC
Lucker: The Apple Inn – www.theappleinnlucker.com – 01668 213824
Ellingham: The Packhorse Inn – www.packhorseinn-ellingham.co.uk – 01665 589252

Not a lot of people know that... the place-name Lucker derives from the old English word for the palm or hollow of one's hand. Knowing that might come in handy one day.

START/END
Seahouses
PARKING:
Centrally located car park.
Charges apply

Alternative START/END
Bamburgh
PARKING:
The main all-day car park on Links Road at the foot of Bamburgh Castle is FREE.

Ordnance Survey maps:
Explorer 340 –
Holy Island & Bamburgh
Landranger 75 – Berwick-upon-Tweed

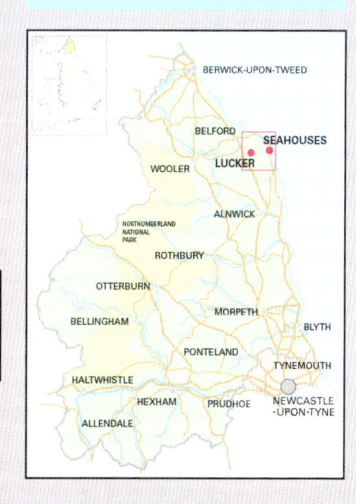

47

Total distance	29 km loop
	31 km Seahouses spur
	30 km Bamburgh spur
Total ascent / descent	246 metres

48

Bamburgh
Castle
Islestone
B1342
Mus
The Friars
Friary (rems of)
Hotel
PC
Dunes
B1340
B1341
Red Barns
Budle
Waren Mill
Settlement
Dukesfield
Greenhill Fm
Outchester
Spindlestone
Glororum
Burton
Fowberry
Monks Ho
New Shoreston
Shorest Hall
Humbleton Hill
Bradford
Goldenhill
Bradford Kaims
Cuckerpool Burn
Springhill
West Field F
Waren Burn
Adderstone Grange
Hoppen Hall
Newhouses
Elford
Pasturehill
Lucker
PH
Lucker South Fm
Embleton's Bog
Newham Hall
dismtd rly
Hill Crest
East Fleetham
Settlement
Coldrife Fm
West Fleetham
Ratchwood (ruin)
Henhill
High Hill
Newham
Priestsdean Burn
Birchwood Hall
Hagg Dean
Newham Hagg
Crutch Bog
Newstead
Newham Bldgs
Chathill
Tughall Covert
The Nest
Commonflat
Hall
Ellingham
Preston
Tower
South Broomfield
Wandylaw
Wood Cott
Dogberry Plantation

Road 11

Wooler. © Graeme Peacock

Wooler, Heatherslaw & Lowick Loop

DISTANCE: 45.4 km / 28.4 miles   **GRADE: Moderate**

SUMMARY: This longer, bi-directional route is a fairly gentle loop ascending and descending almost 500 m spread over the whole ride. You can choose to start at, and return back to, Wooler or start and end at Doddington. Ford, Heatherslaw and Etal are close together and each is well worth a visit – do read up on their fascinating history.

Probably best ridden clockwise to gradually gain what height there is. The route follows 20 km of the *Pennine Cycleway* (NCN Route 68) for the outward leg as you ride across the Milfield Plain. It then follows minor roads to Lowick, where it heads very pleasantly south down an old Roman Road which is why it is so straight. A short link brings you back to lovely old Weetwood Bridge.

ROUTE NOTES

① **TAKE EXTRA CARE** when crossing the A697

② Occasionally, traffic on the B6348 NE of Wooler can be fast.

③ Occasionally, traffic on the B6525 south of Doddington can be fast.

LOOS & BREWS:

Wooler: choice of public houses, cafés and restaurants / WC

Ford: The Old Dairy tea-room (opposite Ford Castle) – 01890 820325 & 01289 302658

Heatherslaw Mill tea-room: 01890 820737 / WC

Etal: public house; Lavender tea-rooms – 01890 820777

Bowsden: Black Bull Inn – 01289 388661

Lowick: The White Swan Inn – www.thewhiteswanlowick.co.uk – 01289 388248; village store

Doddington: ice cream freezer honesty box – www.doddingtondairy.co.uk

START/END
Wooler
PARKING: the route heads out and back along Brewery Road. The Peth is a steep hill which separates the start / end of the route from three free parking locations

Alternative START/END
Doddington
PARKING: at Doddington (limited)

INFORMATION:
www.ford-and-etal.co.uk
www.wooler.org.uk

Ordnance Survey maps:
Explorer 340 – Holy Island & Bamburgh
Explorer 339 – Kelso, Coldstream & Lower Tweed Valley
Landranger 75 – Berwick-upon-Tweed
Landranger 74 – Kelso & Coldstream

Limited parking
START/END

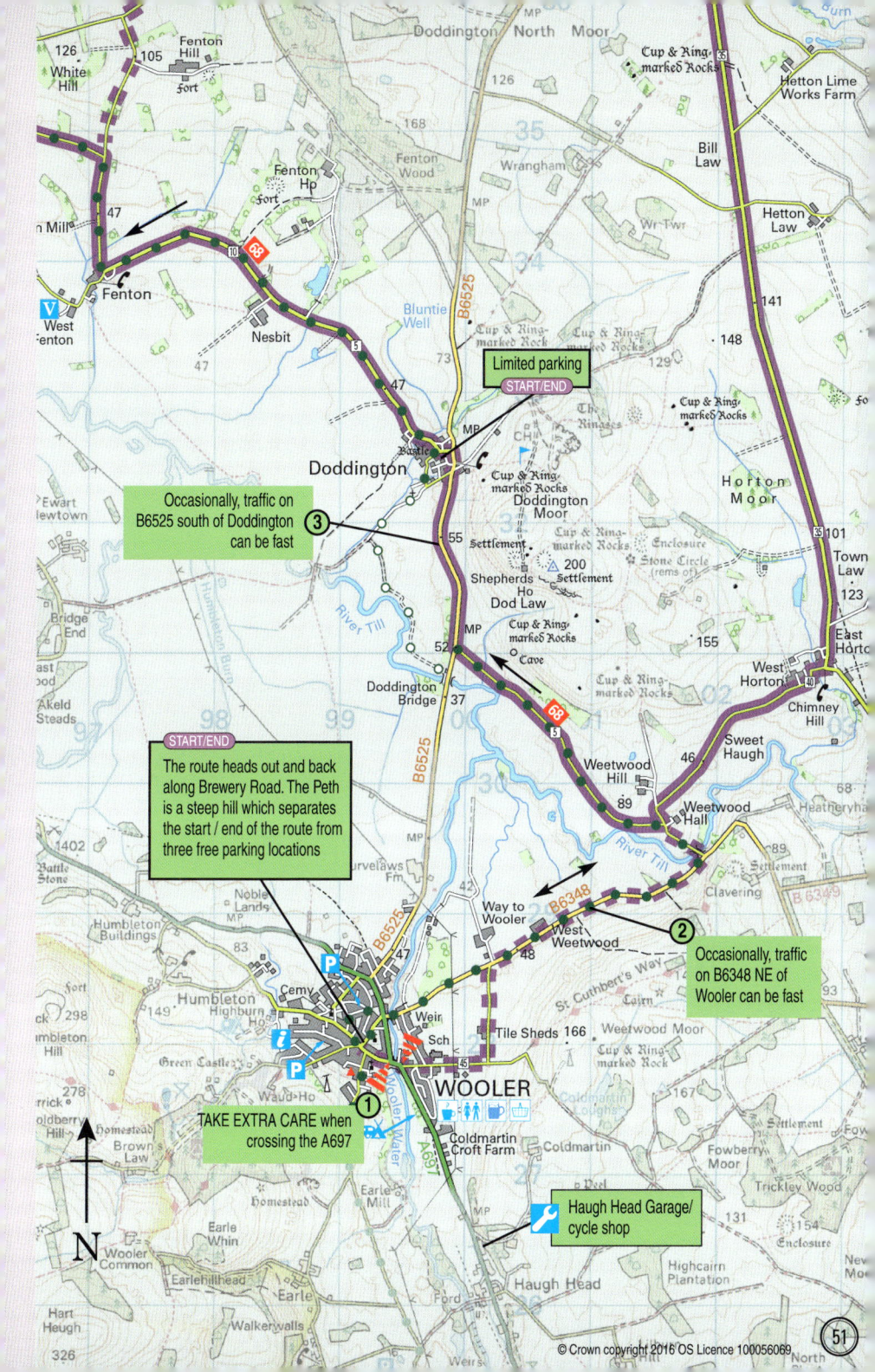

Occasionally, traffic on B6525 south of Doddington can be fast ③

START/END
The route heads out and back along Brewery Road. The Peth is a steep hill which separates the start / end of the route from three free parking locations

Occasionally, traffic on B6348 NE of Wooler can be fast ②

TAKE EXTRA CARE when crossing the A697 ①

Haugh Head Garage/ cycle shop

North Northumberland is rich in cup-and-ring sites which are a form of Prehistoric rock art; Doddington Moor is one of the best places to find them.

SHORT ROUTE

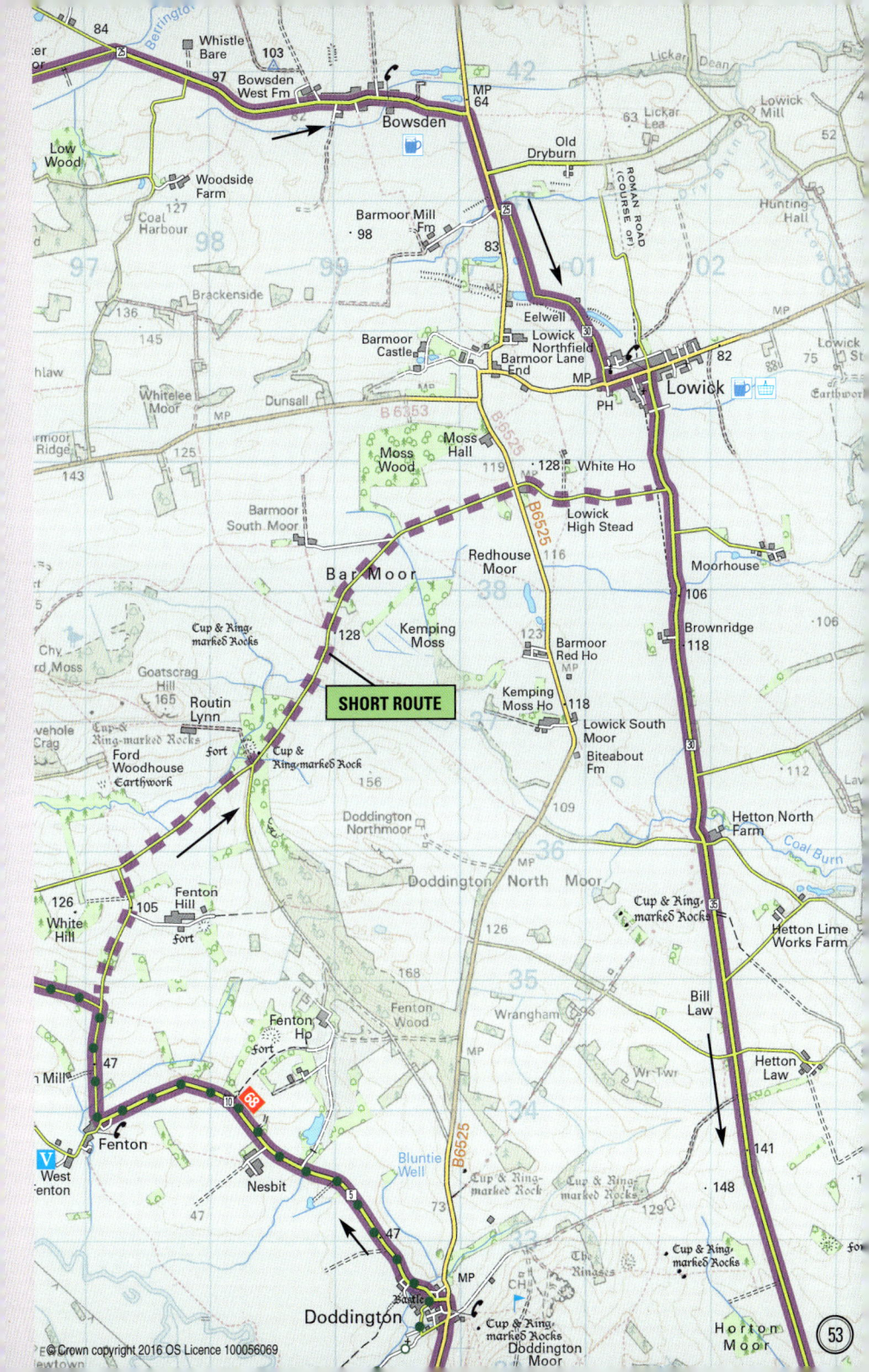

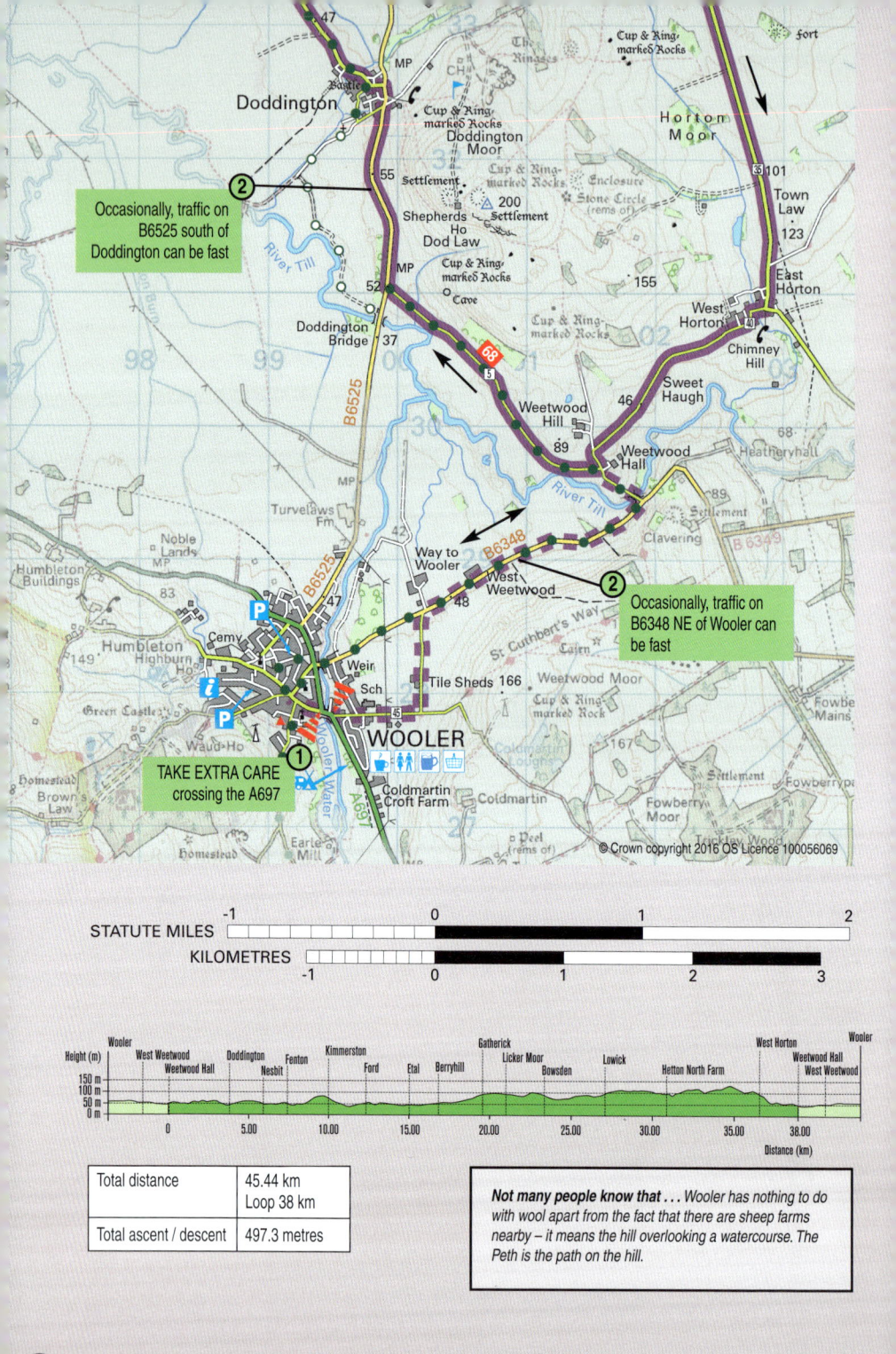

Occasionally, traffic on B6525 south of Doddington can be fast

Occasionally, traffic on B6348 NE of Wooler can be fast

TAKE EXTRA CARE crossing the A697

© Crown copyright 2016 OS Licence 100056069

Total distance	45.44 km
	Loop 38 km
Total ascent / descent	497.3 metres

Not many people know that ... Wooler has nothing to do with wool apart from the fact that there are sheep farms nearby – it means the hill overlooking a watercourse. The Peth is the path on the hill.

54

Road 12

Ford Castle and Church as seen from the route

Milfield, Heatherslaw & Mindrum Loop

DISTANCE: 35 km / 22 miles **GRADE: Moderate**

SUMMARY: North Northumberland is a wonderful place to cycle in and this route is a good example of how true that is. With the Cheviots as a backdrop, the terrain to the north is fairly flat and this loop takes best advantage of the Milfield Plain before gradually increasing undulations take you to the final descent back to the start. The A697 has to be negotiated twice but both crossing points are acceptably safe if you cycle carefully and positively.

The route begins on the A697 in the 30 mph limit until the left turn on to the Milfield Plain. The *Pennine Cycleway* (NCN Route 68) is soon joined at Fenton as far as Heatherslaw and though just a tad off route and slightly uphill, Ford is well worth popping into if you have the time. Re-crossing the A697 at Crookham needs care but the visibility is good, so be patient and wait until it's safe to cross. Keep an eye out for the concrete garden features on your right as you cycle through Branxton. From there to Kilham is easy-going but soon after expect to gently gain some height to West Flodden crossroads, after which it's all downhill to the A697 for the short distance into Milfield.

ROUTE NOTES:

The A697 splits this route but both interfaces are acceptably safe if you pay attention and cycle positively.

① **TAKE EXTRA CARE** through Crookham.
② **TAKE EXTRA CARE** at junction, just to north of Milfield and through Milfield.

LOOS & BREWS:

Milfield: Café Maelmin – 01668 216323
Ford: The Old Dairy tea-room (opposite Ford Castle) – 01890 820325 & 01289 302658
Crookham: Bluebell Inn – www.bluebellcrookham.co.uk – 01890 820789
Heatherslaw Mill tea-room: 01890 820737 / WC
Etal: public house; Lavender tea-rooms – 01890 820777

START/END
Milfield

FREE PARKING: to the rear of the village or at the Wood Henge car park just past the road junction to the south of Milfield
www.maelmin.org.uk

INFORMATION:
www.ford-and-etal.co.uk

Ordnance Survey maps:
Explorer 339 – Kelso, Coldstream & Lower Tweed Valley

Landranger 74 – Kelso & Coldstream

55

Spur to / from Etal

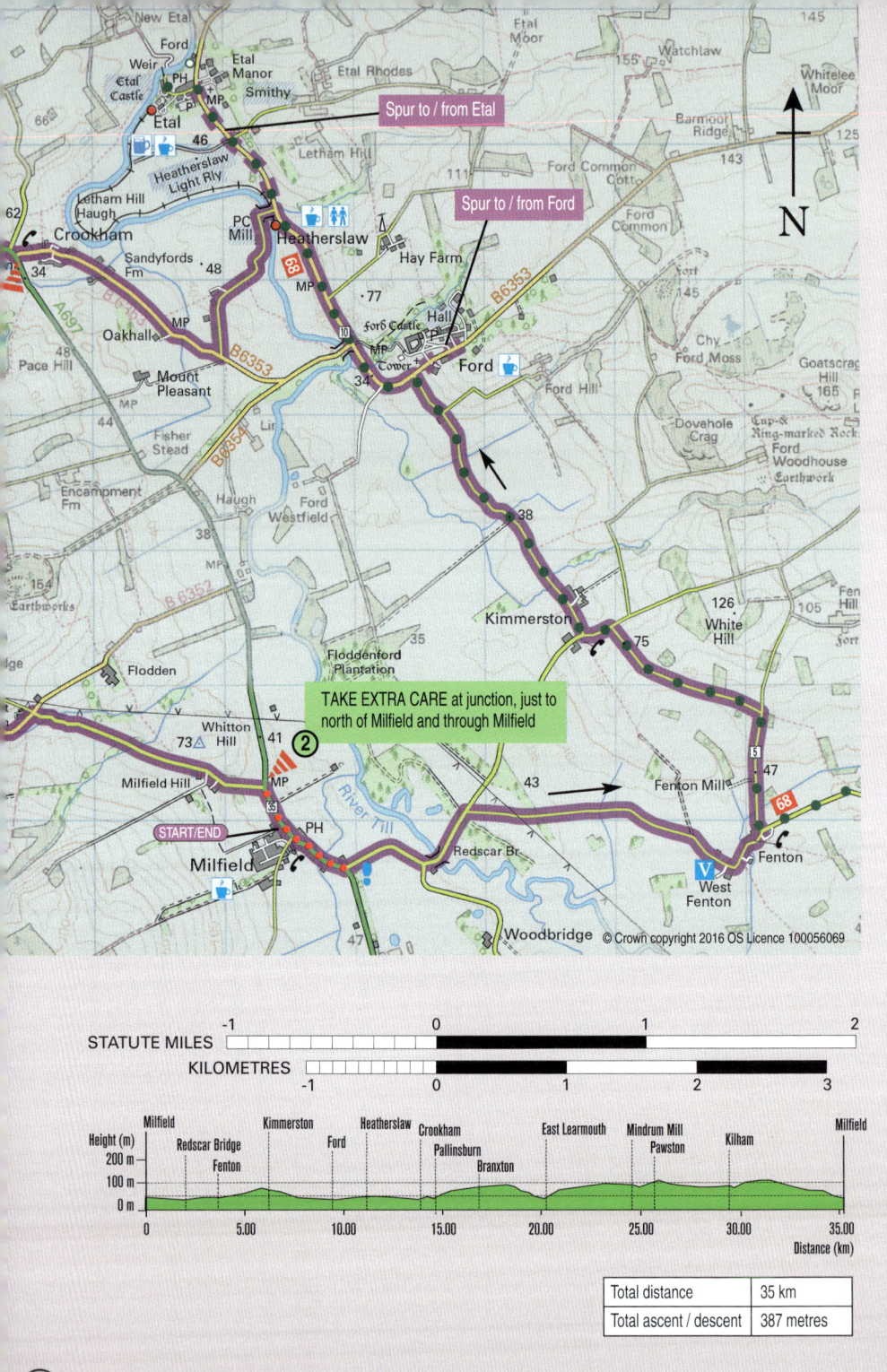

Spur to / from Ford

TAKE EXTRA CARE at junction, just to north of Milfield and through Milfield

START/END

© Crown copyright 2016 OS Licence 100056069

STATUTE MILES
KILOMETRES

Total distance	35 km
Total ascent / descent	387 metres

TAKE EXTRA CARE crossing A697

Not many people know that... the battle of Flodden Field, which took place on 9 September 1513, was one of the bloodiest battles in British history. The Anglo-Scottish clash proved a devastating defeat for the Scots who lost 10,000 men.

Flodden memorial.
Photo: Paul Barlow,
Creative Commons

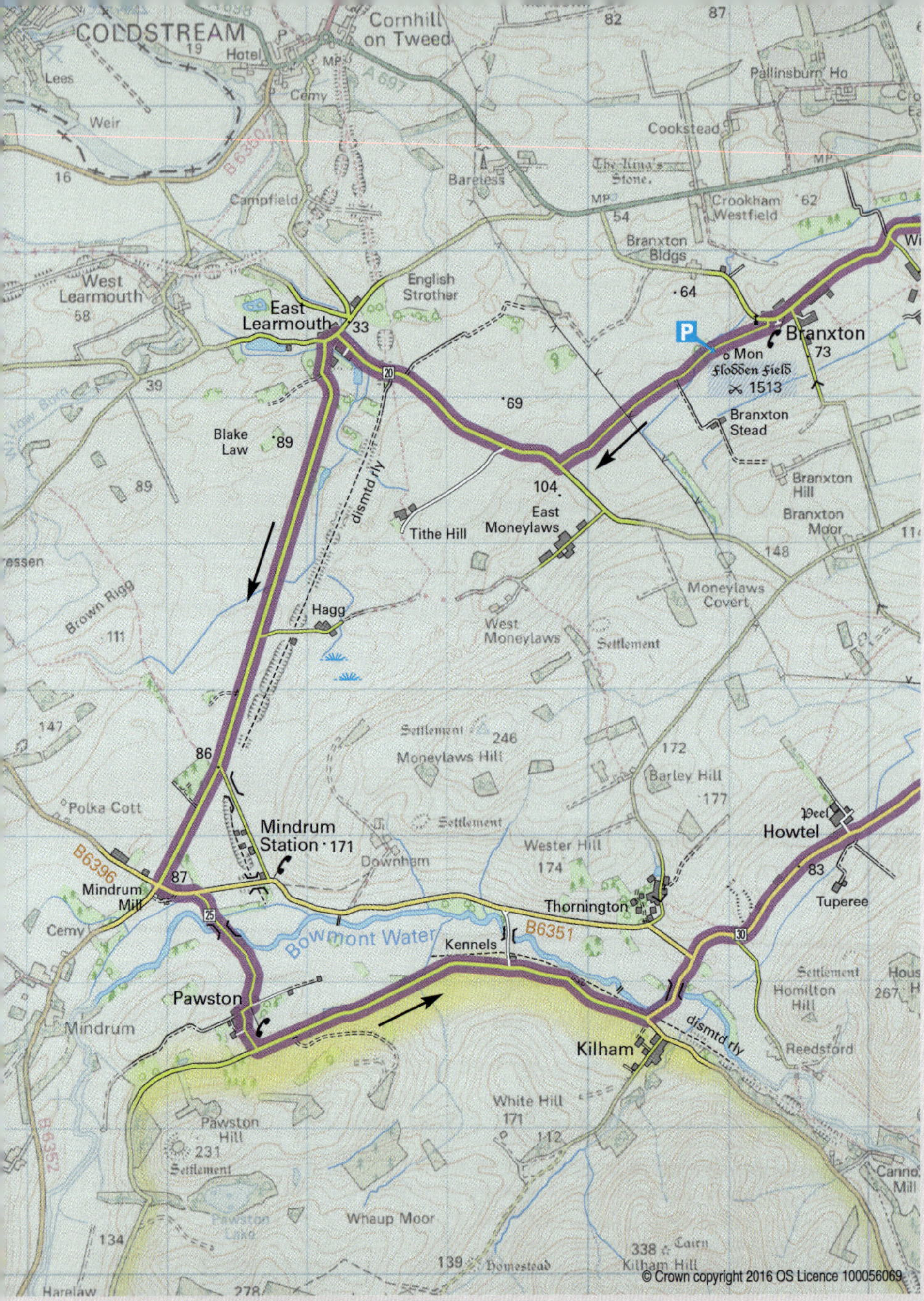
COLDSTREAM
Cornhill on Tweed
Hotel
Lees
Weir
Cemy
A697
B6350
Campfield
Bareless
The King's Stone
Pallinsburn Ho
Cookstead
Crookham Westfield
Branxton Bldgs
West Learmouth
East Learmouth
English Strother
Branxton
Mon
Flodden Field
1513
Branxton Stead
Branxton Hill
Branxton Moor
Blake Law
dismtd rly
Tithe Hill
East Moneylaws
Moneylaws Covert
Brown Rigg
Hagg
West Moneylaws
Settlement
Moneylaws Hill
Barley Hill
Polka Cott
Mindrum Station
Downham
Wester Hill
Howtel
Peel
Tuperee
B6396
Mindrum Mill
Thornington
Cemy
Bowmont Water
Kennels
B6351
Pawston
Mindrum
Kilham
Homilton Hill
Reedsford
Pawston Hill
White Hill
B6352
Pawston Lake
Whaup Moor
Homestead
Cairn
Kilham Hill
Harelaw

Mountain Bike
10 Easy to Moderate MTB Routes

Mountain Bike Routes (MTBs)

MTB ROUTES CHOSEN FOR THIS BOOK

This section contains a set of 10 carefully researched mountain bike rides, graded from easy to moderate, along legal Rights of Way or Permissive Paths, through stunning Northumberland countryside famous for its big skies and far horizons. By using the map you will enjoy cycling down quiet country lanes, through woods and forests, along sheltered valleys and over rolling hills.

Experience the variety of surfaces from double-width gravel tracks and single-width earth and / or stone paths, to bridleways and old unsurfaced country roads. Use the maps to find mountain bike rides along ancient highways and drove roads. You'll discover parts of Northumberland you didn't know existed.

Caution . . .

- Some route sections may become muddy and slippery in wet weather

- Gates should always be left open or closed as found

- Take care when passing cows with calves and never cycle between mothers and their young as they may attack you

MTB 13

Kielder Water Lakeside Way Loop

A fabulous ride on a fine winter's day

DISTANCE: 39 km / 24.5 miles

GRADE: Moderate

START/END
Tower Knowe
PARKING: fees apply.
Car park at Tower Knowe

Alternative START/END
Visitor Centres or stop-off places accessible from the C200 road along the south side of Kielder Water
PARKING: Visitor Centres have designated car parks and fees apply

INFORMATION:
www.visitkielder.com

Ordnance Survey maps:
Explorer OL42 –
Kielder Water & Forest

Landranger 80 –
Cheviot Hills & Kielder Water

SUMMARY: The first point to note about this scenically beautiful bike ride around Kielder Water is that whilst the reservoir is totally flat, the shared-use, traffic-free track around it is anything but, which is why it hasn't been given an easy grade. Nevertheless, this loop really is worth tackling as in the right conditions at any time of year, it's like cycling in Sweden.

Most people will start this bi-directional route at Tower Knowe or at the dam and take advantage of the Kielder Castle facilities at the half-way point, perhaps making another refreshment stop on the return section. This direction also makes best use of the possible shortcut by ferry during operational times. Either way, be prepared for constant undulations and the possibility of pushing up some of the albeit short uphill slopes if your fitness demands it.

Kielder Water's Lakeside Way is one of Northumberland's classic bike rides and is hugely scenic. There are no difficulties and the surface never changes – just don't underestimate its length. Do take this advice on board and allow plenty of time to complete the full circuit, perhaps literally if you decide to catch the ferry. And remember the north shore section is surprisingly remote for quite a distance.

LOOS & BREWS:
Tea-rooms:
Café on the Water. Visitor Centre and WC at Tower Knowe
NE48 1BX – 01434 240 436

Kielder Castle Café. Visitor Centre and WC / NE48 1ER – 01434 250209

Leaplish Waterside Park. NE48 1BT – 01434 251000

Public Houses:
The Boat Inn Restaurant and Bar at Leaplish Waterside Park

The Anglers Arms in Kielder village NE48 1ER – 01434 250072
Don't forget to check opening times as they vary seasonally.

Car park at north end of the dam / WC

IMPORTANT

It is possible to cycle only part of the Lakeside Way by catching the 'Osprey', the Kielder Water ferry which runs as shown on the route map. Tickets can be purchased on board subject to space or in advance at Leaplish Waterside Park or Tower Knowe Visitor Centre. Please check with reception at Leaplish Waterside Park (01434 251 000) when booking as times and prices may be subject to change.

Not many people know that . . .
Kielder Water is the largest artificial lake in the United Kingdom by capacity and is surrounded by Kielder Forest, the largest man-made woodland in Europe. The reservoir is owned by Northumbrian Water and holds 200 billion litres of water.

Mobile phone signal unpredictable

Expect to share the dam road with vehicles

© Crown copyright 2016 OS Licence 100056069

WARNING: Though classified as National Cycle Network, this increasingly remote trans forest route is a mix of stony double tracks and one section of narrow stony singletrack; it is definitely NOT suitable for normal road bikes.

Mobile phone signal unpredictable

ROUTE NOTES

1. Expect to share the dam road with vehicles
2. Mobile phone signal unpredictable

© Crown copyright 2016 OS Licence 100056069

Total Distance	39.22 km
Total ascent / descent	697.7 metres

The route profile is exaggerated due to the scale – there are no mountains on the route!

63

MTB 14

On The Osprey

The Osprey: Kielder Loop

DISTANCE: 20.5 km / 12.7 miles

GRADE: Moderate

START/END
Kielder Castle

SUMMARY: *The Osprey* mountain bike trail is the latest addition to the family of Kielder trails and is the only route in this guide published in its own right. It starts at Kielder Castle and heads up the Forest Drive to the first of several sections of sweeping singletrack as it turns along Kielder Burn and climbs into the forest. The trail links back on to the Lakeside Way on forest road or, for the more adventurous, via a wooden bridge over Plashetts Burn at Wainhope. This section provides an exhilarating decent on singletrack with breathtaking views of the Lakeside Way.

The Osprey trail has been designed as a cross country trail for riders who love a blast and also for riders just starting out on moderate standard (blue) grade trails. It is the next grade up from the Lakeside Way on which it finishes. Do stop by on your way past and see Silvas Capitalis (a play on the Latin for forest head), a giant timber head, just one of the art & architecture pieces along the Lakeside Way.

As with all trails in Kielder, please be fully prepared for riding in remote environments and come properly equipped. The weather can change rapidly and small equipment failures can quickly turn into a more serious situation. Always let somebody know where you are going and when you are due back.

PARKING:
Kielder Castle (parking fee contributes to trail maintenance).

INFORMATION:
www.visitkielder.com

Ordnance Survey maps:
Explorer OL42 –
Kielder Water & Forest

Landranger 80 –
Cheviot Hills & Kielder Water

ROUTE NOTES

(1) Do not rely on having a mobile phone signal.

LOOS & BREWS:
Tea-rooms:
Kielder Castle Café. Visitor Centre and WC / NE48 1ER – 01434 250209

The Anglers Arms in Kielder village NE48 1ER – 01434 250072
Don't forget to check opening times as they vary seasonally.

Total Distance	20.5 km
Total ascent / descent	439 metres

65

MTB 15

The old miner's track near Acomb

Hexham, Acomb & St Oswald's Loop

DISTANCE: 12.3 km / 7.5 miles   **GRADE: Moderate**

START/END
St John Lee: FREE PARKING: St John Lee Church (car park may be busy Sunday mornings or during church events)

Alternative START/END
Hexham - Tyne Green Country Park
FREE PARKING: at the far end in the parking area opposite Café Enna; toilets on approach.

SUMMARY: *Hexham, Acomb & St Oswald's Loop* with an optional link to/from Hexham is the main star here. It's classified as moderate but only because the route ascends some 185 m above the Tyne Valley, albeit gently. There are two possible start points – one at Tyne Green and the other at St John Lee Church. The latter misses out having to cross the Tyne Bridge at Hexham and it also misses out the Hermitage bridleway which is a pity – please see parking limits at St John Lee in the parking section.

This loop just stops short of being a figure of eight. Quiet, gently sloping minor roads take you to the sandy lonnen (lane) which becomes tarmac at Codlaw Hill Farm. Join the B6318 Military Road for a short way then turn left on to the quiet narrow lane which leads to Fallowfield Farm. From there a double-width track bridleway with fine views of the Tyne Valley links very pleasantly on to minor roads that will drop you into Acomb. Turn left at a decorative pant (drinking fountain) and descend the old miner's track to cross an attractive stone bridge. The bridleway then inclines up past Riding Farm's smart buildings, before detouring to picturesque St John Lee Church and the optional return route to Hexham.

INFORMATION:
www.visithexham.net
www.visitnorthumberland.com/hexham

Ordnance Survey maps:
Explorer OL43 – Hadrian's Wall
Landranger 87 – Hexham & Haltwhistle

ROUTE NOTES:

(1) Cycle single file along the B6318 Military Road and stay alert for fast traffic.

(2) **TAKE EXTRA CARE** crossing the Tyne Bridge at Hexham and use the footway adjacent to Rotary Way to access the Hermitage Bridleway turning.

LOOS & BREWS:

Hexham: wide choice of public houses, cafés, restaurants and shops / WC
Café Enna, Tyne Green – www.cafeenna.co.uk – 01434 608154

Acomb: The Miners Arms, Main Street – www.theminersacomb.com – 01434 603909

The Sun Inn, Main Street – www.sun-inn-acomb.co.uk – 01434 602934; village shop

66

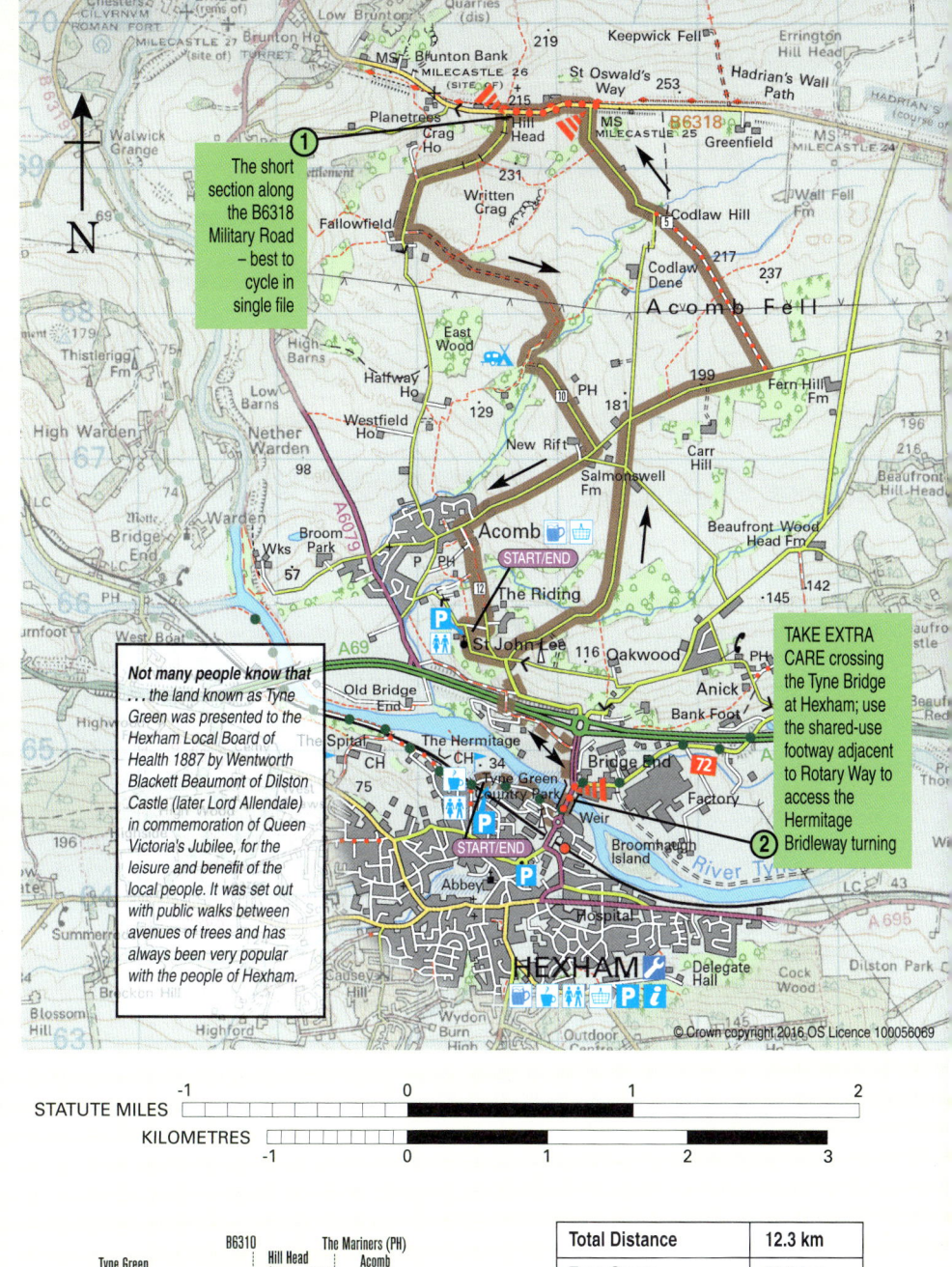

① The short section along the B6318 Military Road – best to cycle in single file

Not many people know that ... the land known as Tyne Green was presented to the Hexham Local Board of Health 1887 by Wentworth Blackett Beaumont of Dilston Castle (later Lord Allendale) in commemoration of Queen Victoria's Jubilee, for the leisure and benefit of the local people. It was set out with public walks between avenues of trees and has always been very popular with the people of Hexham.

② TAKE EXTRA CARE crossing the Tyne Bridge at Hexham; use the shared-use footway adjacent to Rotary Way to access the Hermitage Bridleway turning

© Crown copyright 2016 OS Licence 100056069

Total Distance	12.3 km
Tyne Green	14.3 km
Total ascent / descent (Tyne Green)	255 metres

67

MTB 16

Matfen Hall's original carriage drive

The Stamfordham & Matfen Loop

DISTANCE: 27.75 km / 17 miles   **GRADE:** Easy

SUMMARY: Being close to Newcastle, Stamfordham and Matfen are popular villages with road cyclists as the approach roads are level and there are good refreshment stops. This area isn't as popular with mountain bikers because MTB routes aren't thick on the ground in that locale, but the easy *Stamfordham & Matfen Loop* provides a very pleasant ride out for those happy to mix easy tracks with quiet minor roads. Though technically an easy route, the full loop will test the stamina of averagely-fit cyclists, hence the shortcut which creates two smaller loops.

This route is peppered with too many heritage sites to mention but the main locations are Matfen Hall, ancient East Matfen Village, Wilton Hall Castle, Hadrian's Wall and Vallum, Cheeseburn Grange and Heugh ancient village earthworks. Both Matfen and Stamfordham are bursting with history. *The Stamfordham & Matfen Loop* is best ridden anticlockwise only because the 200 m along the B6318 Military Road is slightly downhill and so can be cycled faster in that direction. The hardest section is the gentle ascent up to Spital Farm which you may have to push if the ground is wet, but dry or wet, the horses will be pleased to see you.

LOOS & BREWS:
Matfen: The Black Bull – www.theblackbullmatfen.co.uk – 01661 855395
Matfen Village Store and tea-room – 01661 886202

High House Farm Brewery & coffee shop:
www.highhousefarmbrewery.co.uk – 01661 886192

Stamfordham: Swinburne Arms – www.swinburnearms.com – 01661 886015

The Swinburne Arms has a long tradition of being a meeting point for Northumbrian cyclists

START/END
Stamfordham
FREE PARKING:
use the lay-by located on the B6309

Alternative START/END
Matfen
FREE PARKING:
in village. Please park with consideration

Ordnance Survey maps:
Explorer 316 –
Newcastle-upon-Tyne
Landranger 88 –
Newcastle-upon-Tyne

ROUTE NOTES:

1 The route from the lodge gates towards Fenwick Shield and on to Matfen is the old drive into Matfen Hall, hence the stone bridges which are sadly now in poor condition.

2 Cycle single file along the B6318 Military Road and stay alert for fast traffic.

10 This section of *The Stamfordham & Matfen Loop* is part of the linear long distance *Reivers Cycle Route* (NCN Route 10) by MTB between St Mary's Lighthouse and Whitehaven.

69

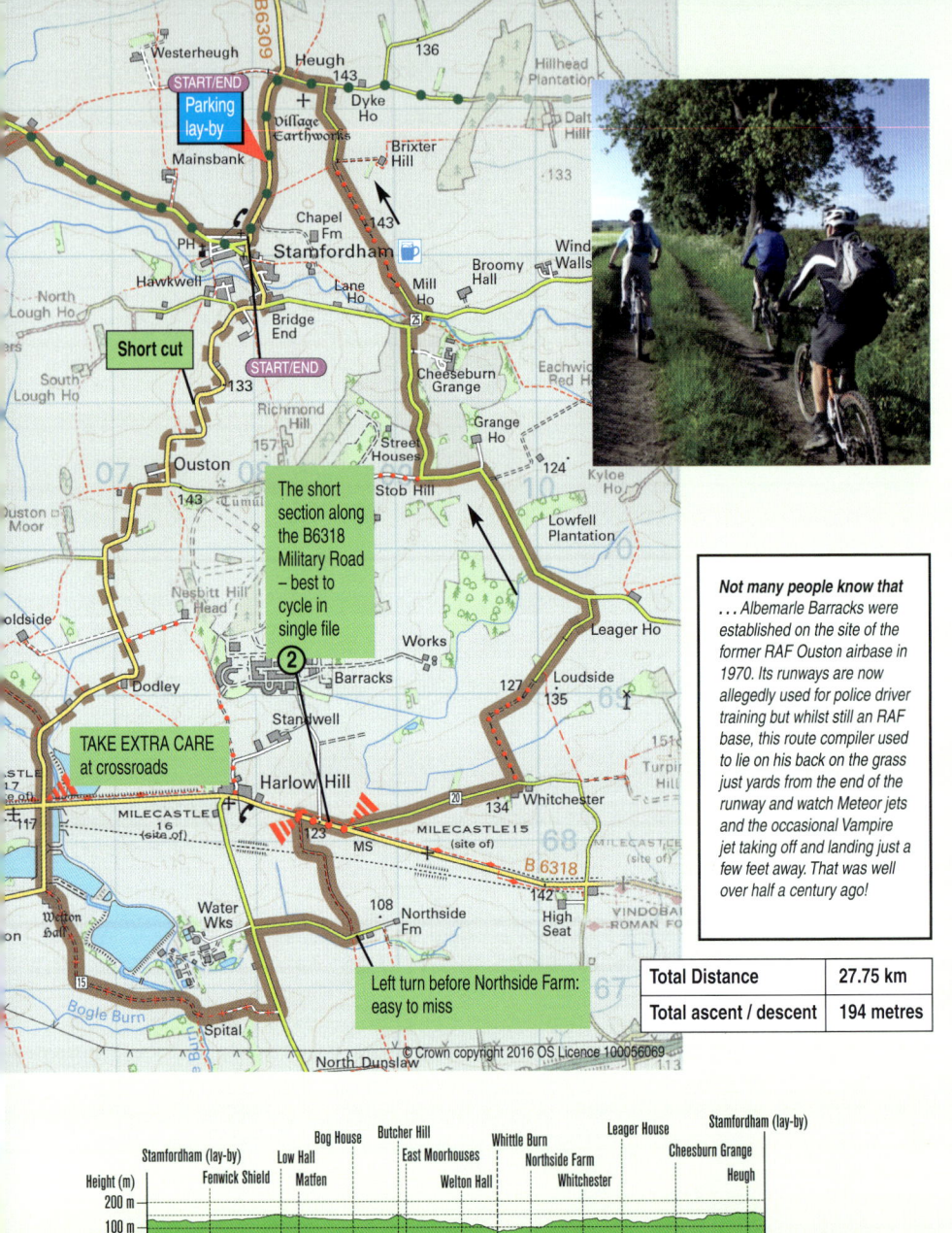

START/END Parking lay-by

Short cut

The short section along the B6318 Military Road – best to cycle in single file

TAKE EXTRA CARE at crossroads

Left turn before Northside Farm: easy to miss

Total Distance	27.75 km
Total ascent / descent	194 metres

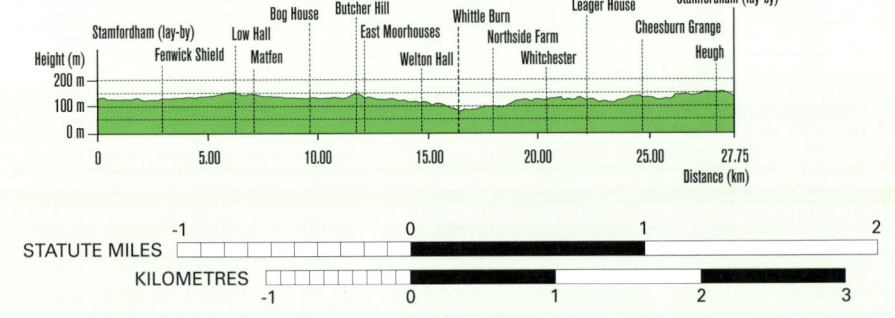

Not many people know that ... Albemarle Barracks were established on the site of the former RAF Ouston airbase in 1970. Its runways are now allegedly used for police driver training but whilst still an RAF base, this route compiler used to lie on his back on the grass just yards from the end of the runway and watch Meteor jets and the occasional Vampire jet taking off and landing just a few feet away. That was well over half a century ago!

70

MTB 17

Cycling this loop in November

Prudhoe & Heddon-on-the-Wall Loop

DISTANCE: 27 km / 17 miles   **GRADE:** Moderate

START/END
Low Prudhoe
FREE PARKING: Tyne Riverside Country Park

SUMMARY: Having crossed the River Tyne from Low Prudhoe to Ovingham, this route takes a reasonably gentle, off-road ascent up to the Whittle Dene Reservoir complex before accessing the B6318 Military Road, which it leaves after about 200 m and then threads its way to Heddon-on-the-Wall. We recommend cycling this route clockwise for the descent on-road on to the shared-use rail path alongside the River Tyne. This popular, flat, traffic-free track to Wylam often requires patience and consideration of other users, particularly during busy times. It is also part of *Hadrian's Cycleway* (NCN Route 72) and used by walkers enjoying the *Hadrian's Wall Path* long-distance walk.

West of Wylam, the track crosses the River Tyne on Points Bridge before continuing along a very pleasant, traffic-free, shared-use riverside section to the Country Park. Again, courtesy towards, and consideration of other users must be the order of the day.

Alternative START/END
Wylam
FREE PARKING: village car park

Tyne Riverside Country Park - Newburn
A short distance to the east of the route.
FREE PARKING: in park car parks

Ordnance Survey maps:
Explorer 316 – Newcastle-upon-Tyne
Landranger 88 – Newcastle-upon-Tyne

ROUTE NOTES:

① Outward the A69 is crossed by a bridge and later re-crossed using the underpass.

② The short section along the B6318 Military Road is soon over – it's best to cycle in single file along here.

③ Pay extra attention to dog walkers on the shared-use riverside path through Wylam.

LOOS & BREWS:
Tyne Riverside Country Park – Low Prudhoe: cafe / WC
Ovingham: two public houses, shop
Heddon-on-the-Wall: The Three Tuns – cyclists welcome, The White Swan, and a tea-room (slightly off route) garage shop / WC
Wylam: choice of public houses, shops and tea-room
George Stephenson's Birthplace: tea-room / WC

Route goes under A69 ①

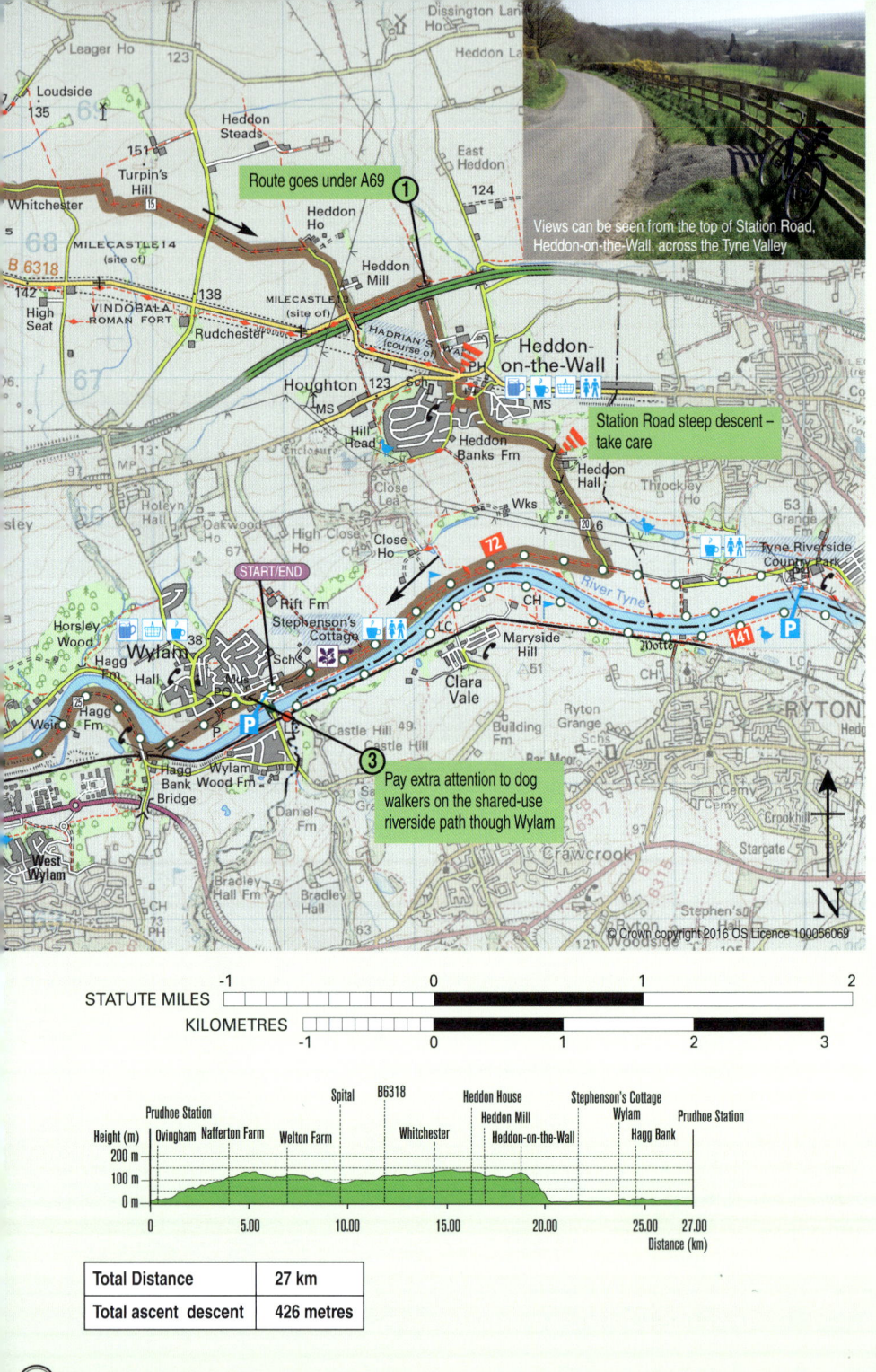

Views can be seen from the top of Station Road, Heddon-on-the-Wall, across the Tyne Valley

Station Road steep descent – take care ②

Pay extra attention to dog walkers on the shared-use riverside path though Wylam ③

Total Distance	27 km
Total ascent descent	426 metres

72

Callouts on map:

- The short section along the B6318 Military Road – best to cycle in single file
- Nafferton Farm to Old Nafferton – can be muddy after wet weather
- Left turn before Northside Farm – easy to miss
- Cross A69 over bridge
- Nafferton Farm – take care through the farm steading and give way to farm activity
- Alternative START/END

© Crown copyright 2016 OS Licence 100056069

Not many people know that... The complex of reservoirs and treatment works straddling the B6318 Military Road form the last stage in the supply of drinking water to Newcastle-upon-Tyne and Gateshead. Completed in 1848, the complex forms part of a series of reservoirs along the A68, which are connected by tunnels and aqueducts, taking water from Catcleugh Reservoir close to the Scottish border via the reservoirs at Colt Crag, Little Swinburne and Hallington.

Near Wylam the route crosses Hagg Bank Bridge, an early example of an arch suspension bridge, built in 1876, its design was ahead of its time.

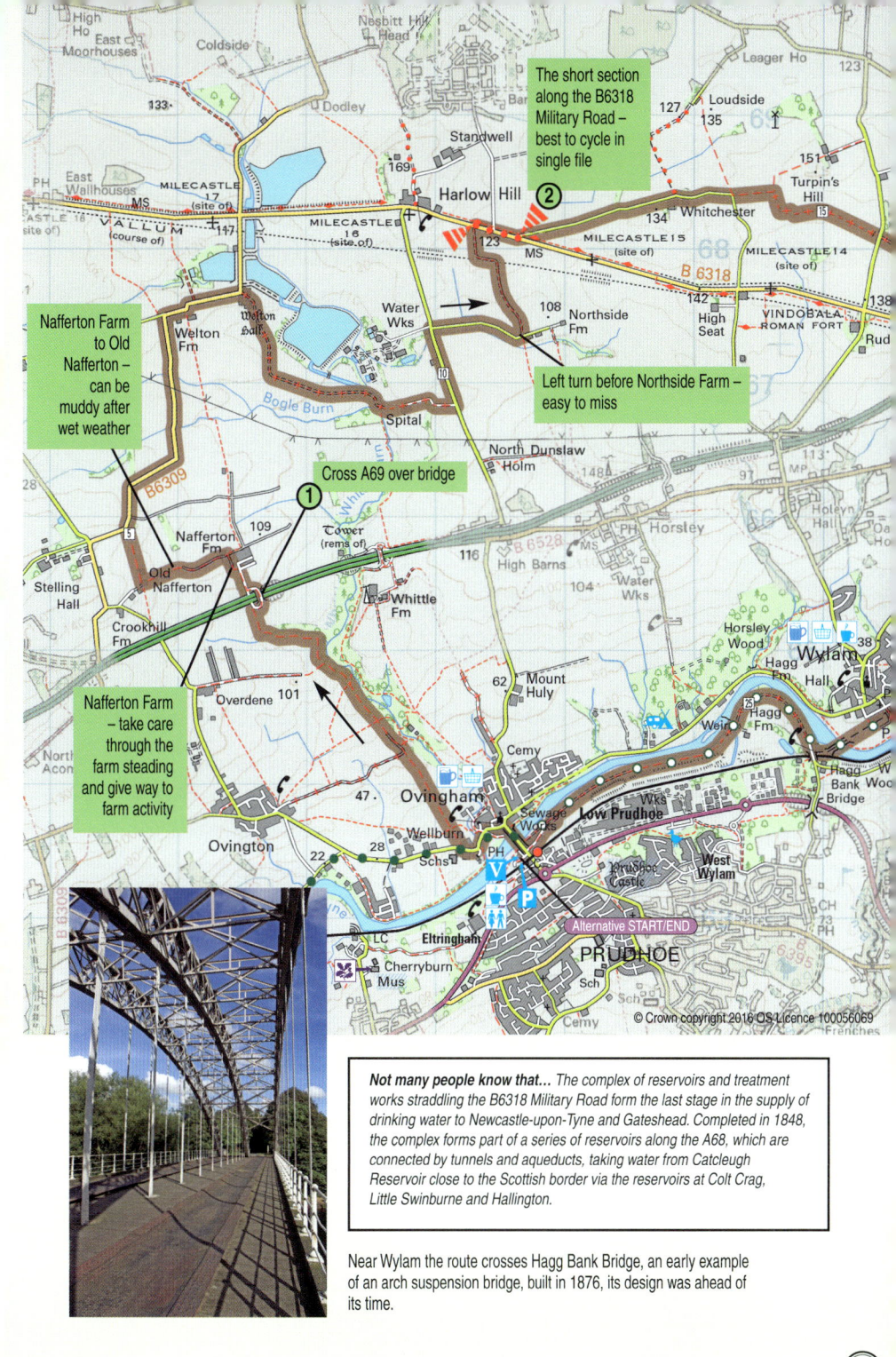

73

Warkworth and Warkworth Castle. © Graeme Peacock

MTB 18

Warkworth & the Coast

DISTANCE: 17 km / 10.6 miles   **GRADE:** Easy

SUMMARY: This relatively short on-road and part off-road loop is best ridden clockwise. It is a fairly level route, rising only slightly as you head inland but enough to make it easier to descend gently to the coast when you get to the north end. Not long after leaving Warkworth, after nearly two miles on a country road, turn right along a double track past Southside Farm. A little over half a mile later, take a left turn along a grassy thinning 'road' which leads to a well-defined double track and a short dog-leg link on to a permissive, grass-covered disused railway track. Turn right to curve down to a small car park and minor road by the railway bridge. Turn right and safely cross the A1068 on to a protected cycle path, where you turn left and very soon right, down a wide track which leads on to a pleasant sandy / grassy bridleway along the top of the dunes. Follow this to join a robust dirt track which zig-zags back to the A1068. Keep left along an even wider dirt track back to the start.

ROUTE NOTES:

(1) **TAKE EXTRA CARE** when crossing the A1068.

LOOS & BREWS:
Warkworth: choice of public houses, cafés, restaurants and shops / WC

> *Not many people know that ...* the spiky grass you see growing on sand dunes is called Marram Grass and plays a vital role in stabilising sand dunes; its fibrous, matted roots bind the sand together. Well-adapted to a harsh life at the coast, its glossy, rolled-up leaves protect it from drying out.

START/END
Warkworth
FREE PARKING: new town car park
Warkworth Dunes Picnic Site
PARKING: car park / WC
Warkworth Castle Car Park - small charge to all visitors (including members) refunded upon admission to the castle

Alternative START/END
Alnmouth
PARKING: village car park

INFORMATION:
www.warkworth.co.uk

Ordnance Survey maps:
Explorer 332 – Alnwick & Amble
Landranger 81 – Alnwick & Morpeth

Map annotations

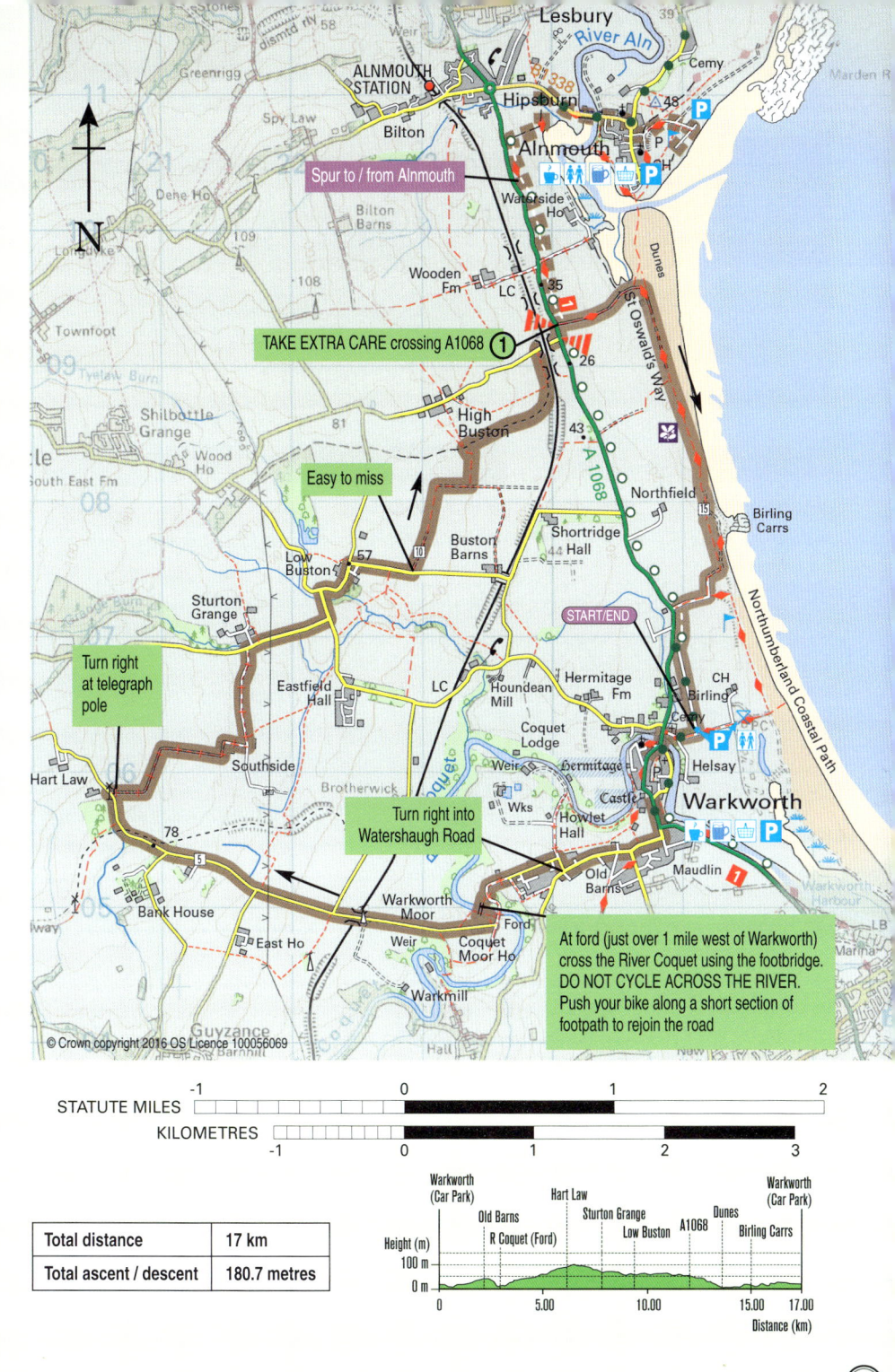

- Spur to / from Alnmouth
- TAKE EXTRA CARE crossing A1068 ①
- Easy to miss
- Turn right at telegraph pole
- Turn right into Watershaugh Road
- START/END
- At ford (just over 1 mile west of Warkworth) cross the River Coquet using the footbridge. DO NOT CYCLE ACROSS THE RIVER. Push your bike along a short section of footpath to rejoin the road

© Crown copyright 2016 OS Licence 100056069

Scale

STATUTE MILES: -1, 0, 1, 2
KILOMETRES: -1, 0, 1, 2, 3

Elevation profile

Warkworth (Car Park) — Old Barns / R Coquet (Ford) — Hart Law — Sturton Grange / Low Buston — A1068 — Dunes / Birling Carrs — Warkworth (Car Park)

Height (m): 0 m – 100 m
Distance (km): 0 – 17.00

Total distance	17 km
Total ascent / descent	180.7 metres

75

MTB 19

The coastal bridleway overlooking Budle Bay close to the turnaround point

Seahouses and Bamburgh

DISTANCE: 20.35 km / 12.7 miles **GRADE: Easy**

START/END
Seahouses
PARKING: centrally located car park, charges apply

SUMMARY: This coastal route combination makes the very best of this very beautiful part of Northumberland between Seahouses and Bamburgh. It is unavoidable to use some roads as the available off-road tracks don't quite connect. The arrows on the map indicate the recommended direction of travel, assuming cyclists start at the main Seahouses car park. From here a short section of rail path leads to a minor road network inland of the coast to connect with the Fowberry / Greenhill Farm track and the coast road which is followed into Bamburgh. It is well worth including the optional there-and-back spur towards Budle Point. The return route at first along the B1341 leads to a kilometre long bridleway which narrows with side growth in the second half of the summer. A short bridleway track leads to the minor roads which provide the return route back to Seahouses.

Alternative START/END
Bamburgh
PARKING: the main all-day car park on Links Road at the foot of Bamburgh Castle is FREE and recommended for use during peak season rather than the village. There is also a car park opposite the entrance to Red Barnes

Ordnance Survey maps:
Explorer 340 – Holy Island & Bamburgh
Landranger 75 – Berwick-upon-Tweed

ROUTE NOTES:

1. The coastal bridleway crosses Bamburgh golf course. Stay alert if you see golfers playing shots.

2. Turn around when the bridleway becomes very narrow, just before a very steep dip.

NB. Continuing to the B1342 is an option. You can turn right to the next left to Glororum crossroads and rejoin the mapped route but this option is quite hilly. The WW II pill-box, built on the crest of a knoll on the short bridleway north of New Shoreston, is a good view point.

LOOS & BREWS:
Seahouses: choice of public houses, cafés, restaurants and shops / WC
Bamburgh: choice of public houses, cafés, restaurants and shops / WC

Not many people know that ... the farm /hamlet of Glororum was named 'Gloweroerum', meaning 'glower over them', in the Bamburgh parish records of baptisms for 1768. This was once the main crossroads, perhaps an influential landowner lived there keeping a strict eye on his tenants.

② Turn around when the bridleway becomes very narrow, just before a very steep dip

① The coastal bridleway crosses Bamburgh golf course. Stay alert if you see golfers playing shots

Alternative START/END

EXTRA LOOP OPTION

START/END

© Crown copyright 2016 OS Licence 100056069

The WW II pill-box, built on the crest of a knoll on the short bridleway north of New Shoreston, is a good view point.

77

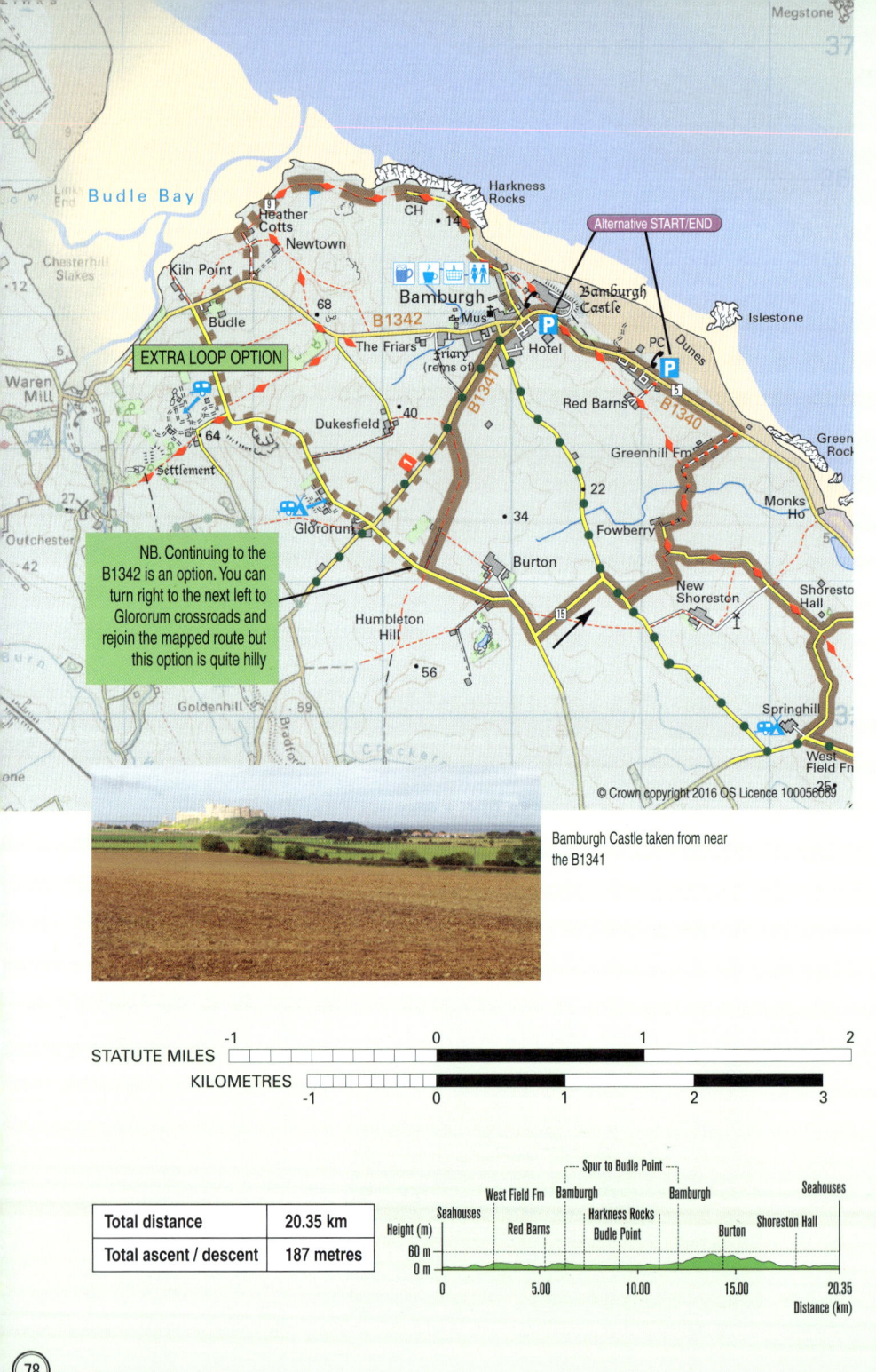

Alternative START/END

EXTRA LOOP OPTION

NB. Continuing to the B1342 is an option. You can turn right to the next left to Glororum crossroads and rejoin the mapped route but this option is quite hilly

Bamburgh Castle taken from near the B1341

© Crown copyright 2016 OS Licence 100056089

STATUTE MILES
KILOMETRES

Total distance	20.35 km
Total ascent / descent	187 metres

MTB 20

Berwick-upon-Tweed to Holy Island Linear

Heading south out of Spittal

DISTANCE: 17 km / 10.6 miles   **GRADE: Easy**

SUMMARY: *The Berwick-upon-Tweed to Holy Island Linear* route is like no other in this book simply because of the setting, the iconic scenery and the coastal situations, so do choose a calm, fine day to ride it. Never rising over 33 m above sea level, the route follows the *Sandstone Way* between the quayside and Beal and is also signposted the *Coast & Castles Cycle Route* (NCN Route 1). In order from the north, follow the coast road to Spittal, before using East Street, then North Greenwich Road and St Helens Terrace to access the promenade. A narrow link path leads to the cliff-top track to Sea House, then a tarmac section parallels Cocklawburn beach. Continue on a shared-use track to the railway bridge and then on tarmac to Beachcomber House, after which a really pleasant track provides the link to the Beal / Holy Island causeway, Greenway.

Holy Island

If you decide to cycle from the mainland to Holy Island and back again as opposed to pre-arranging a lift back to the start, then do check the wind direction and strength. Take special notice that a friendly, off-shore westerly will zoom you across the causeway to the village of Holy Island in no time, but cycling back in a headwind is both energy and time sapping. It goes without saying that you must check the tide timetable before leaving the mainland.

LOOS & BREWS:

Berwick-upon-Tweed: wide choice of public houses, cafés, restaurants and shops / WC

Beal: Barn at Beal – www.barnatbeal.com – 01289 540044

West Mains: Lindisfarne Inn – www.lindisfarneinn.co.uk – 01289 381223

Holy Island: choice of pubs, cafés / WC

START/END
Berwick-upon-Tweed

PARKING: FREE with disc, The Barracks car park saves taking a vehicle through the town but in quiet times there is a car park close to the start /end point

Alternative START/END - Beal
PARKING: Barn at Beal if you provide patronage

INFORMATION:
www.visitnorthumberland.com/berwick-upon-tweed

www.visitberwick.com

www.visitnorthumberland.com/holy-island

www.lindisfarne.org.uk

Ordnance Survey maps:
Explorer 346 – Berwick-upon-Tweed

Explorer 340 – Holy Island & Bamburgh

Landranger 75 – Berwick-upon-Tweed

79

BERWICK-UPON-TWEED

The very old King James I Bridge is a one-way flow in your favour when cycling south

Berwick-upon-Tweed to Holy Island and back is probably enough for less fit cyclists

Cycling cliff-top path near Redshin Cove

© Crown copyright 2016 OS Licence 100056069

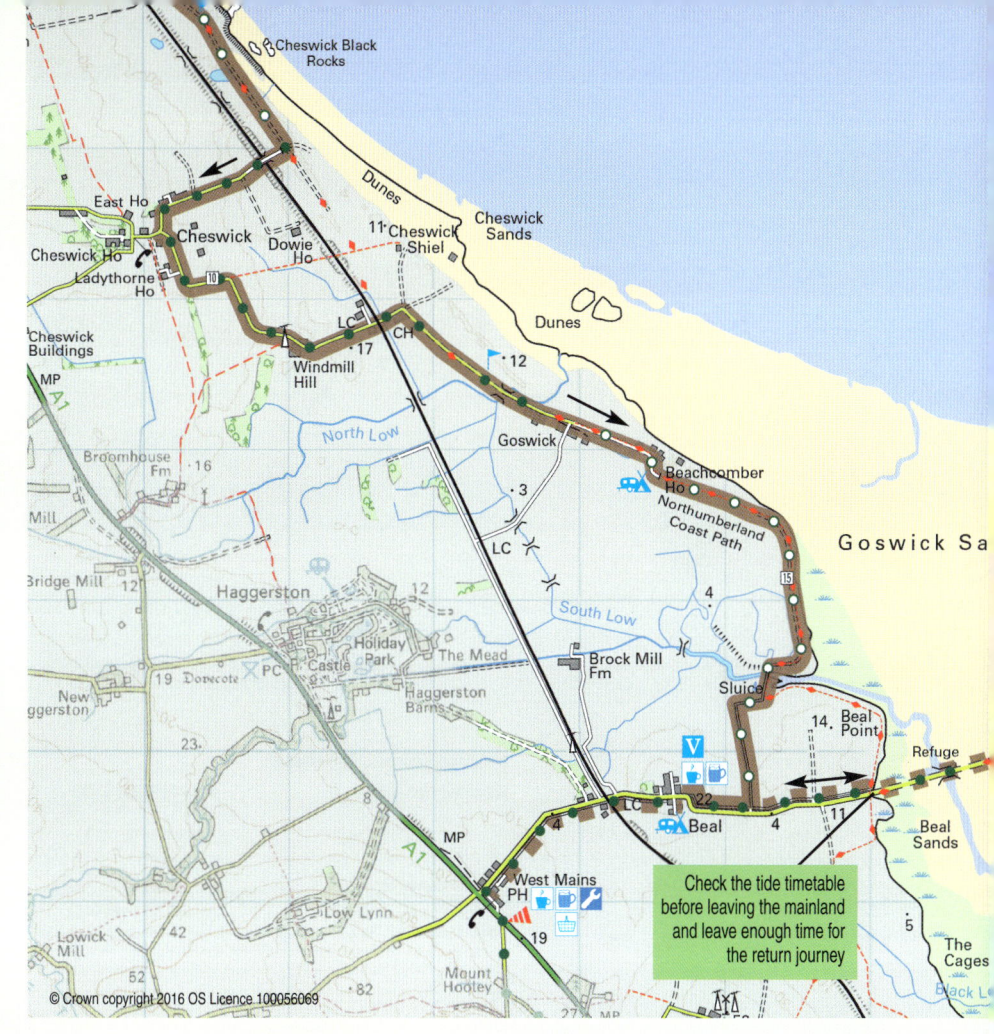

Check the tide timetable before leaving the mainland and leave enough time for the return journey

Not many people know that . . . the artist LS Lowry (1887-1976), famous for his 'matchstick men' paintings of industrial scenes, visited Berwick-upon-Tweed many times from the mid-1930s to the summer before his death in 1976. He was drawn to the town by its fascinating architecture and close proximity to the sea, which inspired him to produce more than twenty paintings and drawings during his visits.

Coastal path near Goswick Sands

81

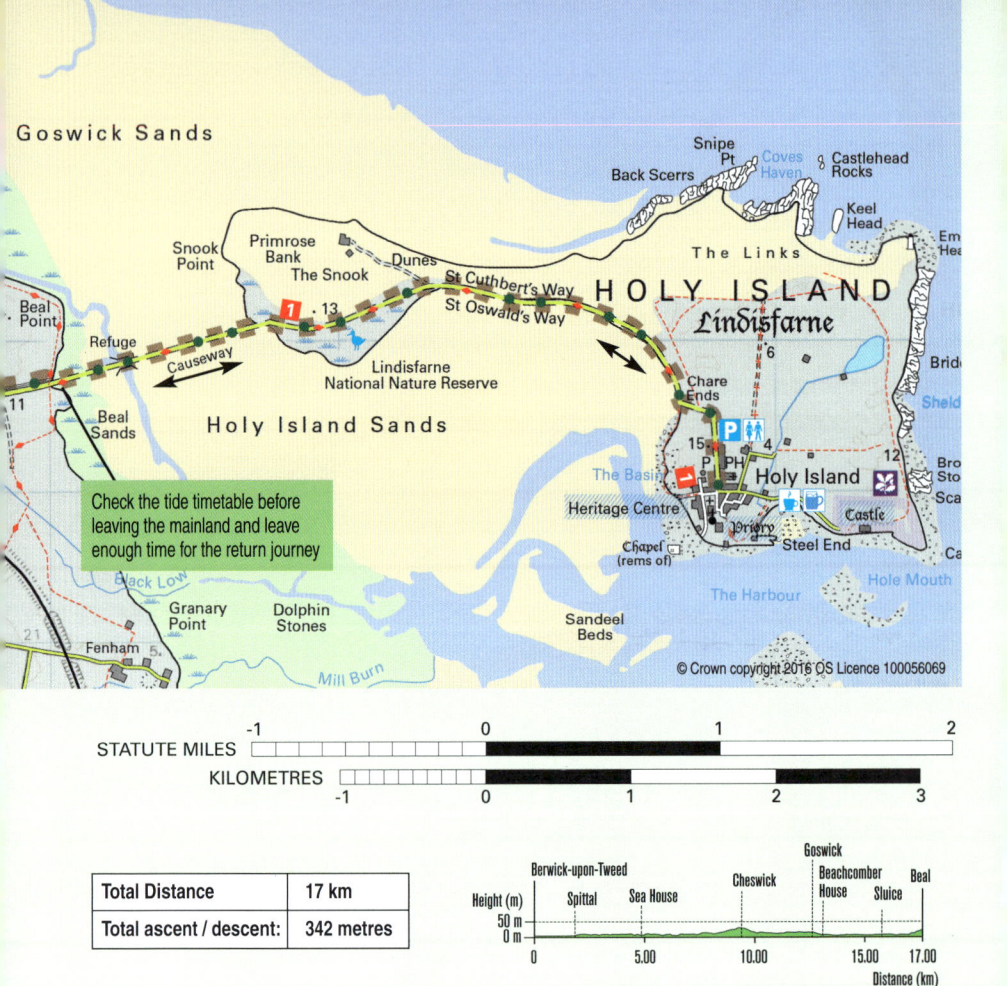

Check the tide timetable before leaving the mainland and leave enough time for the return journey

Total Distance	17 km
Total ascent / descent:	342 metres

Goswick Sands

82

MTB 21

The hidden valley descent to Earle – very pleasant even on a wet day

Wooler & Lilburn Tower Loop

DISTANCE: 17 km / 10.6 miles **GRADE: Moderate**

START/END
Wooler

FREE PARKING:
Padgepool Place at the west end of Wooler main street near the Tourist Information centre www.visitnorthumberland.com/tourist-information-centre/wooler-tourist-information-centre

INFORMATION:
www.wooler.org.uk

Ordnance Survey maps:
Explorer OL16 – Cheviot Hills
Landranger 75 – Berwick-upon-Tweed

SUMMARY: With the expansive rolling Cheviots to the west of Wooler and hilly land immediately to the east, the options for shortish, easy to moderate mountain bike routes based around Wooler are limited. With its choice of two starts, the *Wooler & Lilburn Tower Loop* more than acceptably meets this need. The western option begins with a short, sharp uphill out of Wooler before undulating on narrow tarmac to Brown's Law, after which you may have to push for 500 m. Wooler Common to Earle is a delightful downhill to where it meets the direct option from Wooler. The ongoing route via several Lilburns is easy to follow and the gentle uphill on a section of the *Sandstone Way* **www.sandstoneway.co.uk** from Point 66 is soon over. This becomes a double track which is followed all the way into Wooler. A second shortcut links to this track as shown but probably everyone will opt to ride the full circuit.

ROUTE NOTES

1. You may need to push this section between Brown's Law and Wooler Common.
2. Use footbridge arrowed to ford near Haugh Head.
3. At Haugh Head Farm, cross straight over the A697 **WITH CARE** and go through the gate opposite to continue the route.
4. **TAKE EXTRA CARE** when crossing the A697 in Wooler.

LOOS & BREWS:
Wooler: wide choice of public houses, cafés, restaurants and shops / WC

83

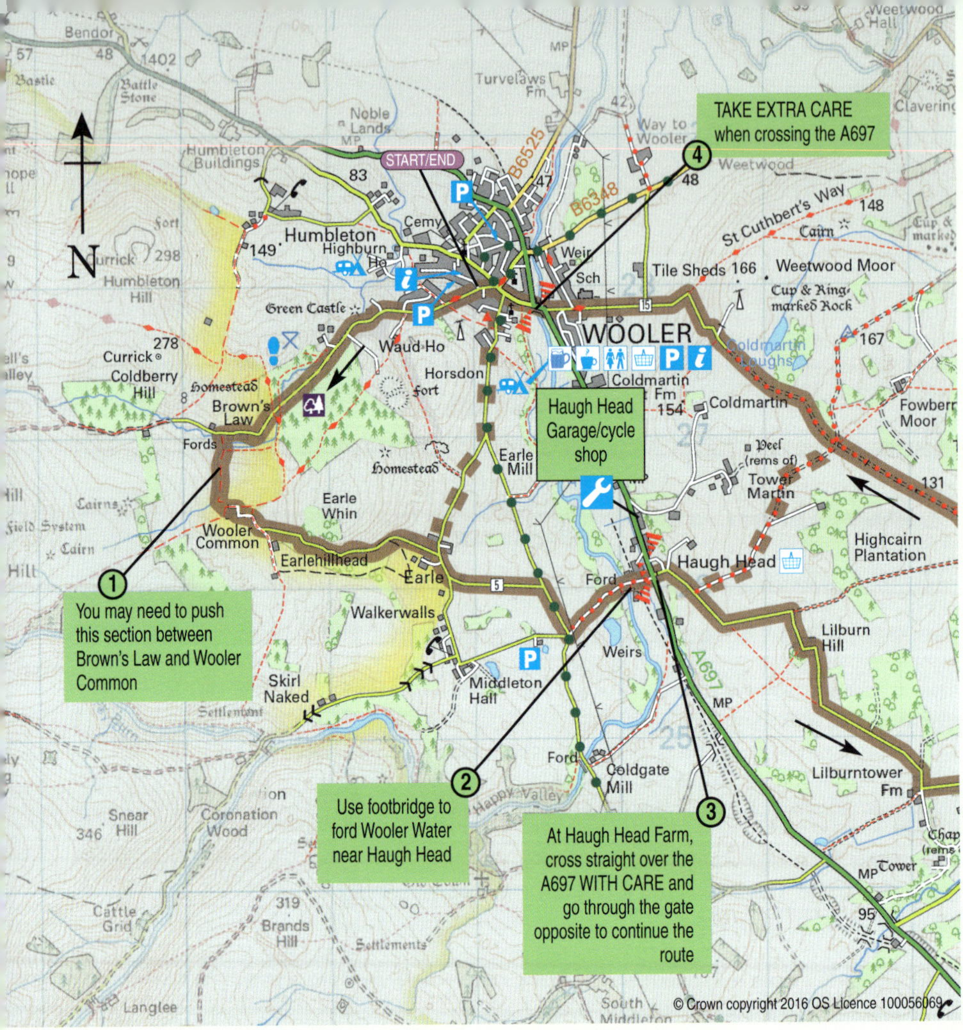

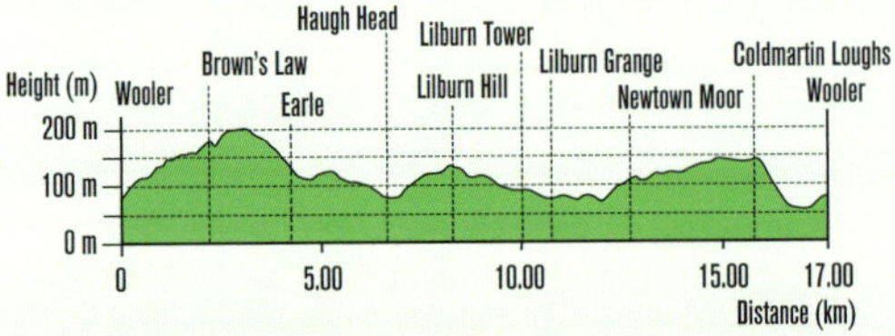

Total Distance	17 km
Total ascent / descent:	381 metres

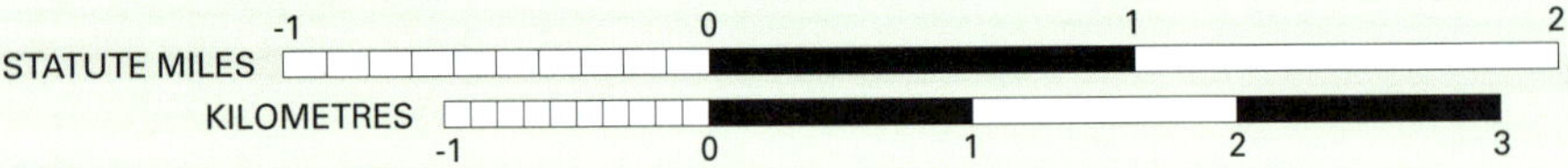

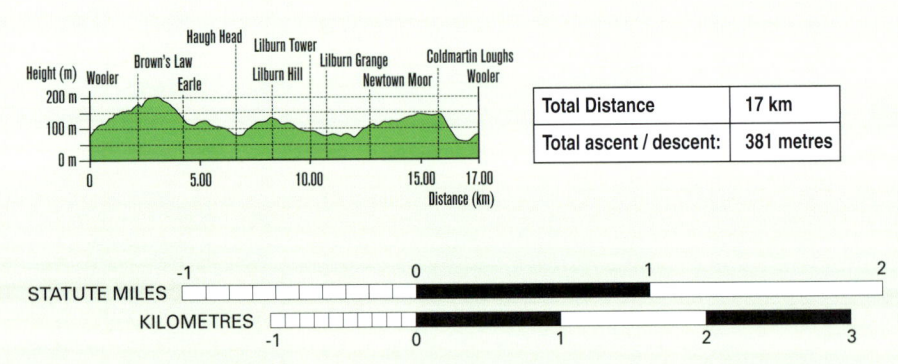

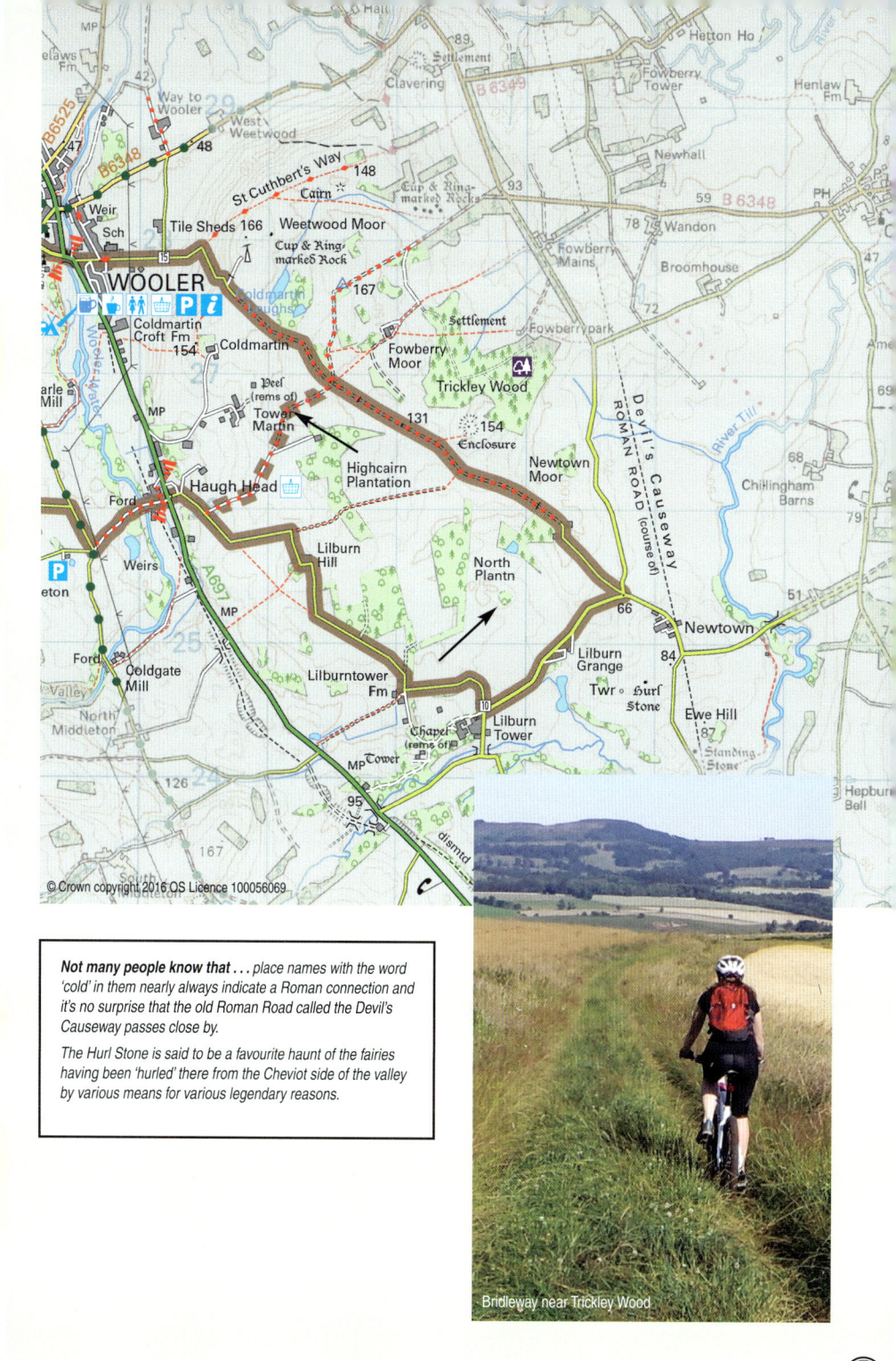

Not many people know that . . . place names with the word 'cold' in them nearly always indicate a Roman connection and it's no surprise that the old Roman Road called the Devil's Causeway passes close by.

The Hurl Stone is said to be a favourite haunt of the fairies having been 'hurled' there from the Cheviot side of the valley by various means for various legendary reasons.

Bridleway near Trickley Wood

MTB 22

Lady's Bridge – perhaps the original wooden bridge was named after Lady Armstrong

Rothbury & Great Tosson MTB Loop

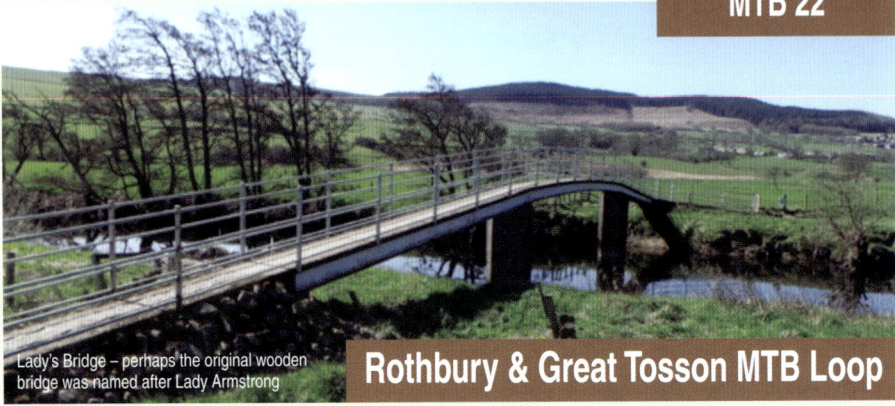

DISTANCE: 11 km / 7 miles   **GRADE: Easy/Moderate**

START/END
Rothbury

FREE PARKING:
Riverside car park as indicated on the route map

INFORMATION:
www.visitnorthumberland.com/rothbury
www.rothbury.co.uk
www.sandstoneway.co.uk

Ordnance Survey maps:
Explorer OL42 – Kielder Water and Forest
Landranger 81 – Alnwick & Morpeth

SUMMARY: Rothbury is a traditional market town in central Northumberland. Known as the Capital of Coquetdale, the town is built from the same sandstone which makes up the rolling hills that surround it. Those same hills limit the cycling opportunities for easy / moderate standard routes but these two routes fall within that grade. The main loop is best cycled clockwise, which means the height is gained acceptably easily early on. Follow the green *Sandstone Way* waymarks between Whitton and the main entrance to the forest via Whitton Hillhead Farm. Only the short section through the wood just before the minor road is moderate grade. Enjoy the expansive views towards the Cheviots before the descent towards the picturesque hamlet of Great Tosson with its ruined tower. Do stop to check out the well preserved lime kiln just before the road fork. Cross the River Coquet using Lady's Bridge, before returning to Rothbury along the tarmacked shared-use path next to the river.

ROUTE NOTES

① **TAKE CARE** descending to the sharp right turn. Make time to stop off at Tosson lime kiln and Tosson Tower where interpretative panels provide background information. It's a long time since wolves were seen on Wolves' Haugh! Cross the River Coquet using Lady's Bridge.

LOOS & BREWS:

Rothbury: wide choice of public houses, cafés and restaurants / WC

Not many people know that . . . the first mention of Rothbury, as far as is known, was around the year 1100 as Routhebiria, perhaps meaning "Routha's town".

86

TAKE CARE descending to the sharp right turn

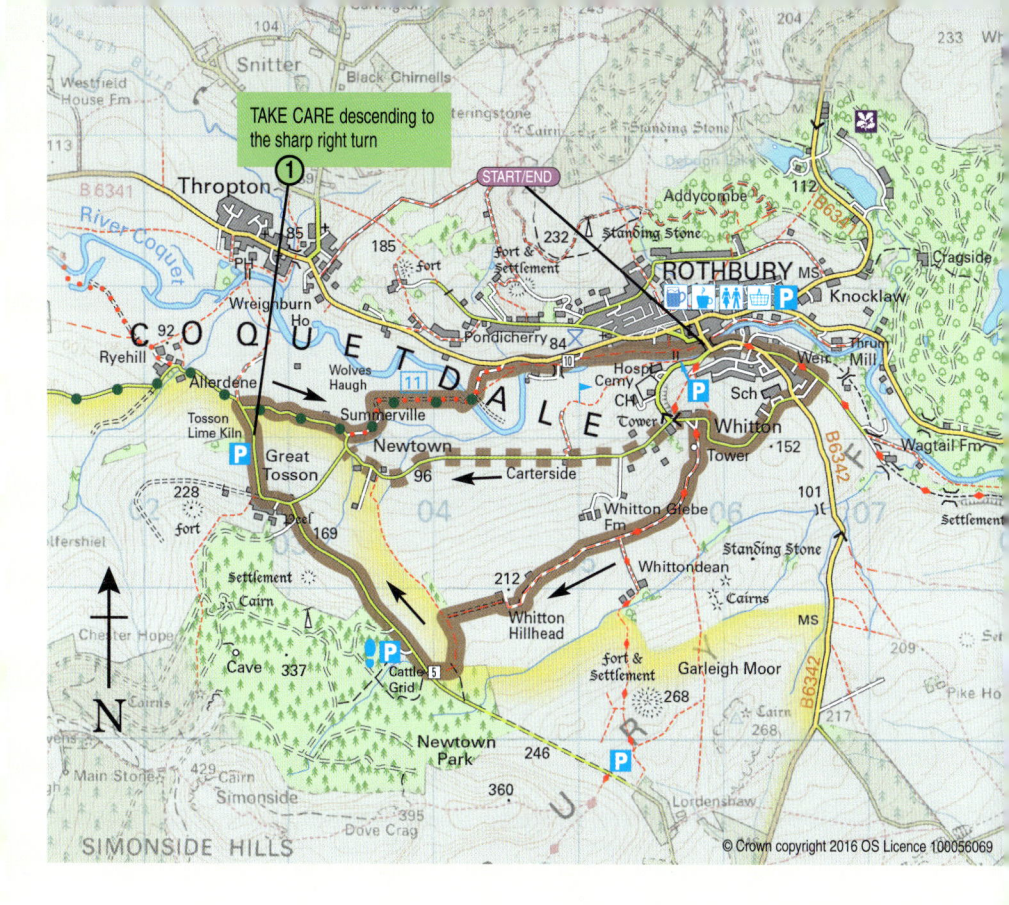

① START/END

Total Distance	11 km
Total ascent / descent:	188 metres

Some people know that . . . the industrialist Lord Armstrong (1810–1900) helped shape modern Rothbury. Many local buildings reflect his Victorian style and prosperity. At the same time, the planting of more than six million trees and shrubs transformed the surrounding landscape. His magnificent home at Cragside was visited by the Shah of Persia in 1889 and the King of Siam in 1897. Now in the care of the National Trust, Cragside is visited by more than 150,000 people annually.

Lady's Bridge – perhaps the original wooden bridge was named after Lady Armstrong.

Thrum Gorge spur

The Thrum Gorge spur is a short 'there and back' route along what used to be called Lover's Walk, past Thrum Mill whose amazing renovation was featured on TV. Beyond the Mill is Thrum Gorge, said to be 23 feet deep and once spanned by a footbridge. The River Coquet's funnelled currents have carved wavy edges on the gorge over many centuries and created an undercut shelf on each side which makes the river unsafe to swim in. In 1880 Jamie Mackay died attempting to jump the gap, which was later blasted to stop repeat attempts. Thrum is a Northumbrian onomatopoeic word meaning "heaving with activity" – an ideal description for this location.

Riverside path to Thrum Gorge

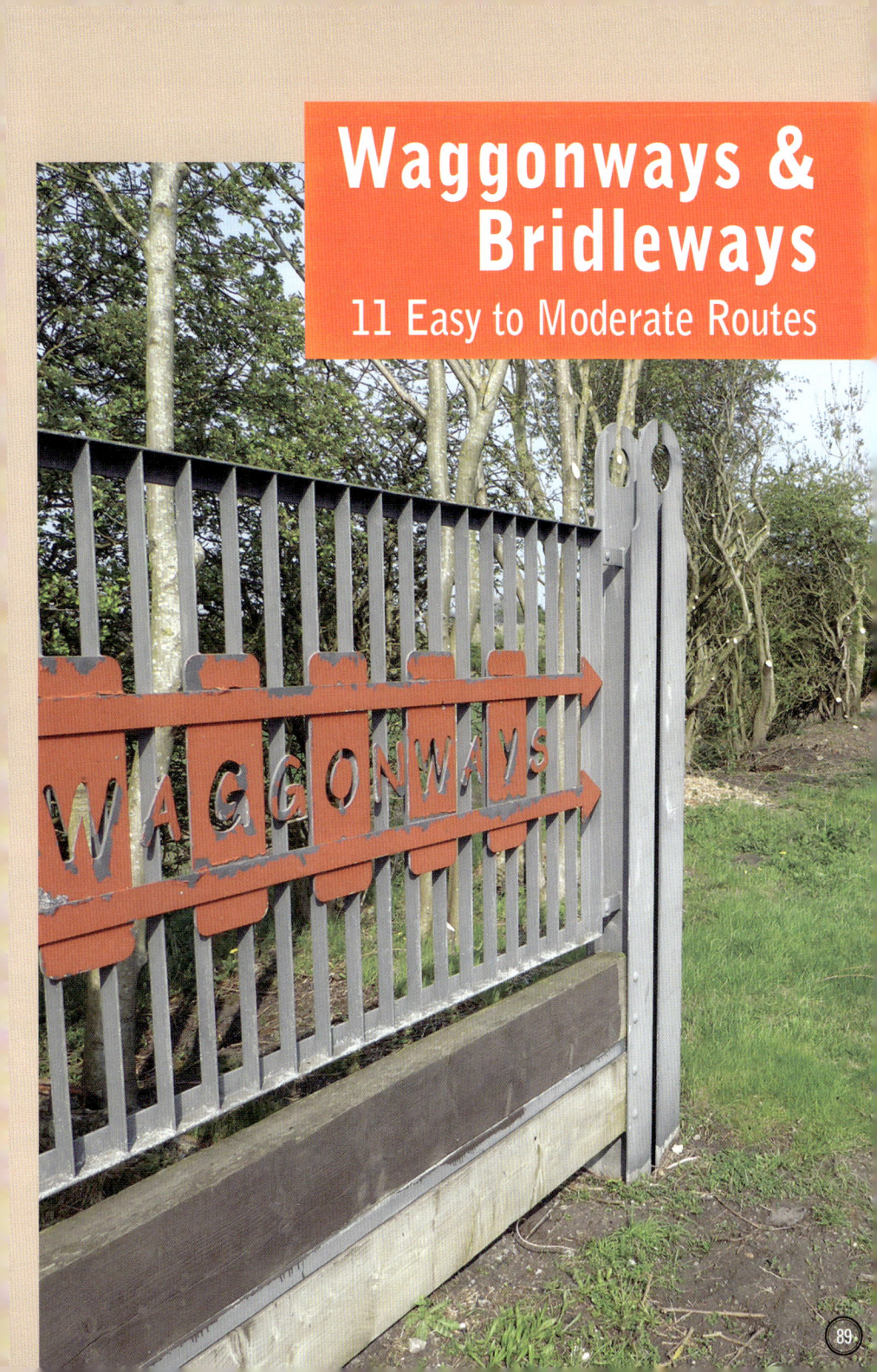

Waggonways & Bridleways

11 Easy to Moderate Routes

Waggonways & Bridleways

WAGGONWAYS are a series of paths that crisscross Tyneside through rural and urban areas, cutting through fields and woodland, between tall hedgerows, past villages and over roads and streams. Originally, waggonways were constructed between the 18th and 20th centuries to transport coal from the inland mines to the River Tyne and to sea ports for export. The early horse-drawn, coal-carrying wagons running on wooden rails were replaced in the 19th century by powerful steam locomotives running on iron rails. These rails were removed in the 1960s and 1970s when the coal mines closed, leaving behind a 30-mile network of restored and traffic-free, almost level waggonways for walkers, horse-riders and cyclists to explore.

This section of the book brings together a carefully researched selection of some of the very best waggonways and bridleways, taking in some minor roads, and occasionally residential streets, to create a series of excellent cycling loops for all abilities to enjoy.

You need to be aware that the planning and construction of new housing estates will inevitably have an effect on some of these routes. However, they cannot be blocked off because Rights of Way have to be protected by law. Some may even be improved as a result.

Caution . . .

- Cyclists must always give way to walkers and horse riders
- Be considerate to dog walkers and avoid frightening animals
- Always slow down and give audible warning of your approach
- Be courteous and give a friendly greeting.

BRIDLEWAYS these are ways "over which the public has a right of way on foot and a right of way on horseback or leading a horse, with or without a right to drive animals along the way." Although Section 30 of the Countryside Act 1968 permits the riding of bicycles on public bridleways, the act says that it "shall not create any obligation to facilitate the use of the bridleway by cyclists". Thus, the right to cycle exists, even though it may be difficult to exercise on occasion, especially in winter.

Biodiversity:

Waggonways and bridleways are invaluable for the conservation of our wildlife as they allow free movement of birds and animals to and from green spaces. These routes are a mixture of hedgerow, scrub and unimproved grassland habitats now rare in North Tyneside.

SAFETY WHEN CYCLING WAGGONWAYS AND BRIDLEWAYS
Cyclists using these are obliged to give way to other users on foot or horseback.

Cyclists should always slow down when passing walkers, politely warn of their presence and stop and give way if in any doubt. Exchanging a friendly greeting goes a long way!

Always expect to meet with dogs, both on and off leads, when cycling on shared use paths.

www.waggonways.co.uk is a good source of information to explore further the waggonway network.

Waggonways & Bridleways 23

Riverside path near Prudhoe

Wylam & Newburn Rail Path Loop

DISTANCE: 19 km / 11.9 miles

GRADE: Easy

Family-friendly route

START/END
Low Prudhoe
FREE PARKING: Low Prudhoe – Tyne Riverside Country Park (south side of the river)

Alternative START/END
Wylam
FREE PARKING: village car park

Newburn
Tyne Riverside Country Park
FREE PARKING: Newburn: Tyne Riverside Country Park

Ordnance Survey maps:
Explorer 316 – Newcastle-upon-Tyne
Landranger 88 – Newcastle-upon-Tyne

SUMMARY: This route closely hugs the River Tyne on almost entirely flat, traffic-free paths which are also popular walking routes, so considerate cycling at all times is necessary. The western third is a wending, traffic-free, 'there-and-back' section with a few gentle undulations which add plenty of interest. The remaining eastern two thirds lie on either side of the River Tyne, to and from Wylam, but provide two quite different experiences. The north side follows the old railway track-bed which this route compiler remembers travelling on by train. The south side track has narrow sections where considerate co-existence with walkers is essential. Undoubtedly, this very pleasant riverside route is ideal for families and less confident cyclists with or without the extension to the Tyne Riverside Country Park at Prudhoe.

ROUTE NOTES:

① Expect to meet with dogs, both on and off leads, when cycling on these shared-use paths.

② The Prudhoe start / end is very close to Prudhoe railway station, where trains carry at least two bikes on a first-come basis.

LOOS & BREWS:
Tyne Riverside Country Park – Low Prudhoe: café / WC
Wylam: choice of public houses, shops and tea-room
George Stephenson's Birthplace: tea-room / WC
Newburn: Newburn Sports Centre, The Keelman public house; shops
Newburn Activity Centre: offers bike hire for individuals and groups
NE15 8ND – Tel: 0191 264 0014

www.waggonways.co.uk
is a good source of information to explore further the waggonway network

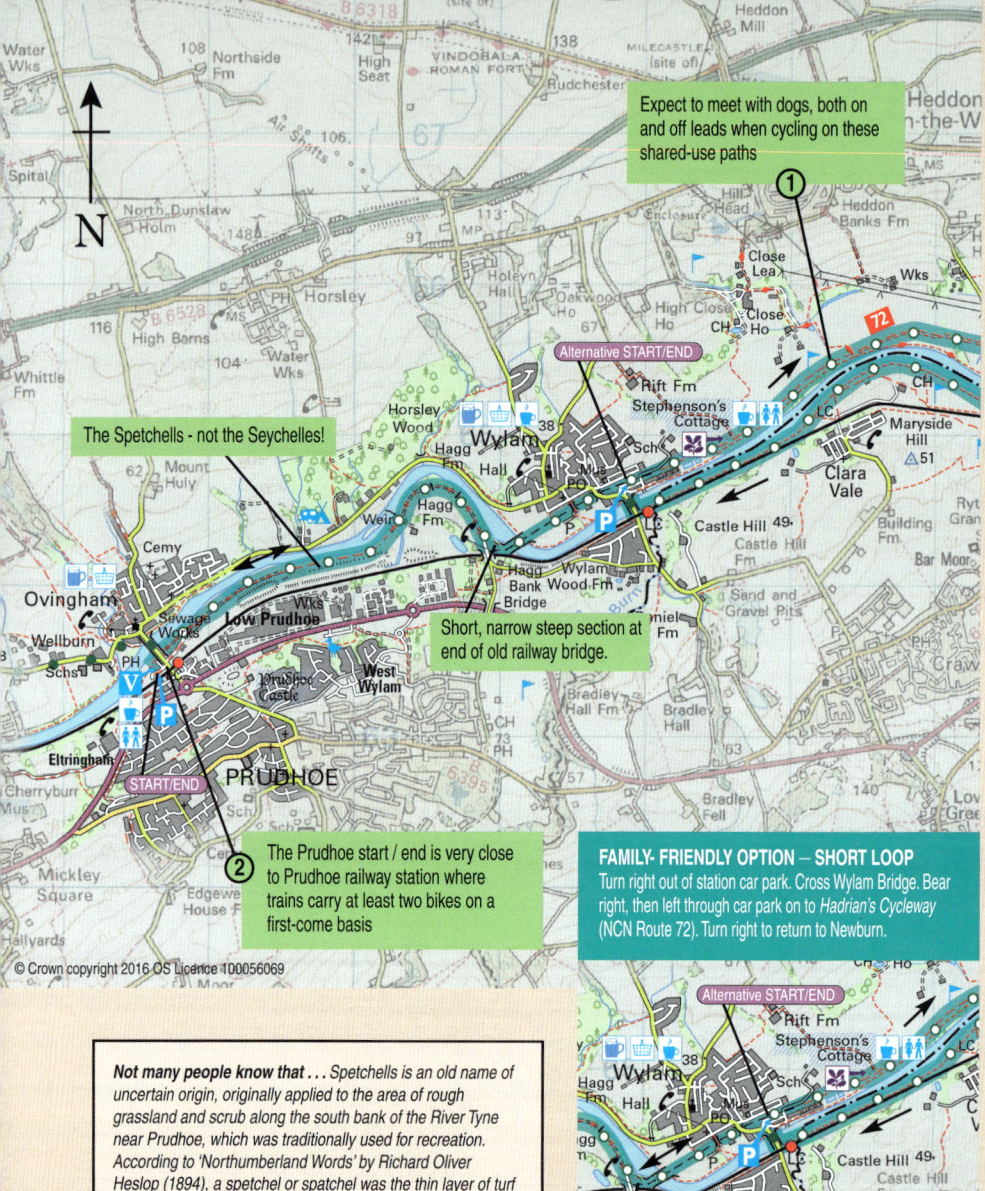

Expect to meet with dogs, both on and off leads when cycling on these shared-use paths

①

The Spetchells - not the Seychelles!

Short, narrow steep section at end of old railway bridge.

② The Prudhoe start / end is very close to Prudhoe railway station where trains carry at least two bikes on a first-come basis

© Crown copyright 2016 OS Licence 100056289

FAMILY- FRIENDLY OPTION – SHORT LOOP
Turn right out of station car park. Cross Wylam Bridge. Bear right, then left through car park on to *Hadrian's Cycleway* (NCN Route 72). Turn right to return to Newburn.

Short, narrow steep section at end of old railway bridge.

© Crown copyright 2016 OS Licence 100056289

FAMILY-FRIENDLY OPTION TO PRUDHOE
Turn right out of station car park. Cross Wylam Bridge. Bear right, then left through car park on to *Hadrian's Cycleway* (NCN Route 72). Turn left to cycle to Prudhoe.

Not many people know that . . . Spetchells is an old name of uncertain origin, originally applied to the area of rough grassland and scrub along the south bank of the River Tyne near Prudhoe, which was traditionally used for recreation. According to 'Northumberland Words' by Richard Oliver Heslop (1894), a spetchel or spatchel was the thin layer of turf laid between horizontal rows of stones used in building a wall ('a stone and spetchel dike').
The name is now associated with the 1 km long mound of calcium carbonate between the River Tyne and the railway, which is the result of industrial waste following the manufacture of ammonium sulphate for fertiliser and explosives during World War II. Wildlife now thrives as this land supports plants typical of the ungrazed chalk grasslands of southern England, and a specialised, chalk-loving species of fauna has also arrived, as well as rare butterflies and moths.

Newburn Bridge: TAKE CARE crossing

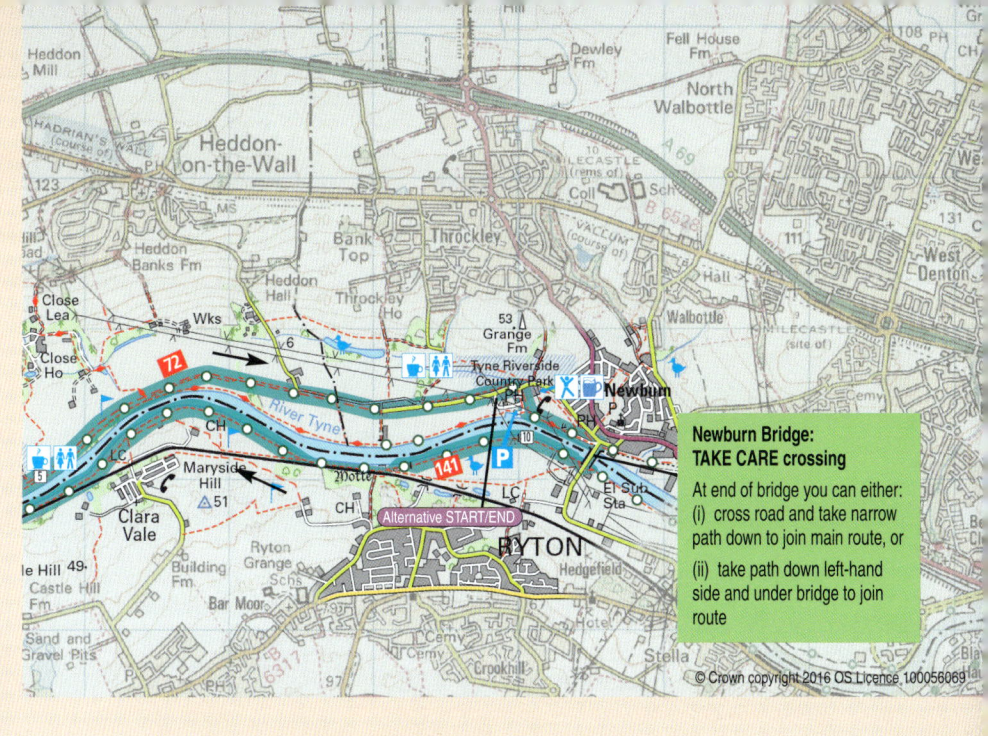

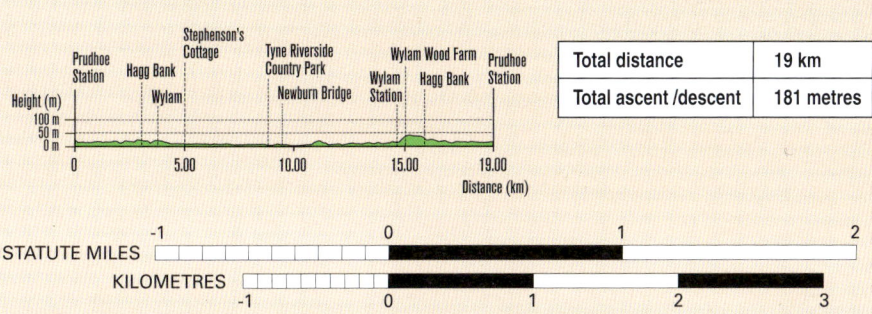

At end of bridge you can either:
(i) cross road and take narrow path down to join main route, or
(ii) take path down left-hand side and under bridge to join route

Total distance	19 km
Total ascent /descent	181 metres

Family-friendly cycling on riverside path between Newburn and Wylam

Waggonways & Bridleways 24

Bridleway, Houghton Farm

Wylam & Newburn Upper Loop

DISTANCE: 21.6 km / 13.5 miles

GRADE: Easy

START/END
Wylam
FREE PARKING: village car park

Family-friendly section

Alternative START/END
Newburn: Tyne Riverside Country Park
FREE PARKING: Newburn – Tyne Riverside Country Park

SUMMARY: *The Wylam & Newburn Upper Loop* is an interesting combination of waggonways, bridleways, converted rail paths and minor roads. Assuming a Wylam start, the route heads northwards up and out of the Tyne Valley on a back road before following the B6528 for just over a kilometre. A mix of different route types zig-zags you to North Walbottle, to access a semi-urban yet pleasantly rural bridleway which heads southwards along an old waggonway before passing under the A69. After a zig-zag across the B6528 and again on an old waggonway, the route continues southwards downhill. On entering an open area, bear right to pass under heavy-duty power lines before joining the *Hadrian's Cycleway* (NCN Route 72). A short link path is easy to miss. Follow this pleasant ride westward, passing close to Newburn Sports Centre which is an optional start.

Ordnance Survey maps:

Explorer 316 – Newcastle-upon-Tyne

Landranger 88 – Newcastle-upon-Tyne

ROUTE NOTES:

(1) Wylam to Houghton Farm is the easiest way to gain height out of the Tyne Valley to access all the fun sections that follow back to the start.

(2) Cross the A6085 with care – cycle on to the grass on the opposite side of the short access road to join a short path next to the fence line leading to a direct crossing point of the main road and the next section of bridleway.

LOOS & BREWS:

Wylam: choice of public houses, shops and tea-room
George Stephenson's Birthplace: tea-room / WC
Newburn: Newburn Sports Centre, The Keelman public house; shops
Newburn Activity Centre; offers bike hire for individuals and groups
Heddon-on-the-Wall: The Three Tuns Inn – cyclists welcome, The White Swan; and a tea-room (slightly off route) garage shop / WC

94

Map annotations

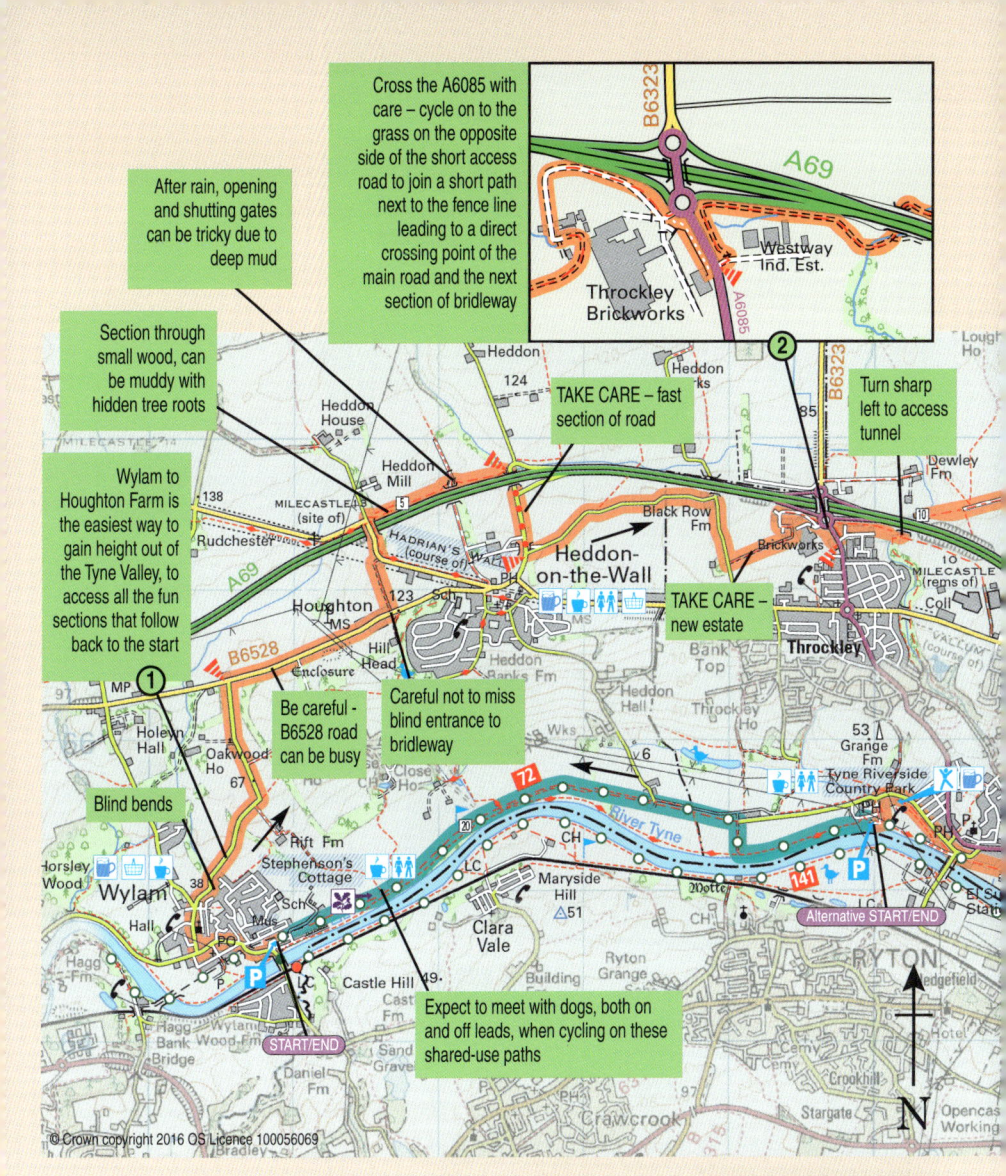

Cross the A6085 with care – cycle on to the grass on the opposite side of the short access road to join a short path next to the fence line leading to a direct crossing point of the main road and the next section of bridleway

After rain, opening and shutting gates can be tricky due to deep mud

Section through small wood, can be muddy with hidden tree roots

TAKE CARE – fast section of road

Turn sharp left to access tunnel

Wylam to Houghton Farm is the easiest way to gain height out of the Tyne Valley, to access all the fun sections that follow back to the start

TAKE CARE – new estate

Be careful - B6528 road can be busy

Careful not to miss blind entrance to bridleway

Blind bends

Expect to meet with dogs, both on and off leads, when cycling on these shared-use paths

START/END

Alternative START/END

© Crown copyright 2016 OS Licence 100056069

Some people know that . . . George Stephenson (1781 – 1848) was the Wylam-born civil and mechanical engineer who built the first public inter-city railway line in the world to use steam locomotives, which is why he became known as the 'Father of the railways'. Stephenson's rail gauge of 4 feet 8 1/2 inches, sometimes known as 'Stephenson gauge' is the standard gauge still used by most of the world's railways.

Cyclists passing Stephenson's Cottage, Wylam

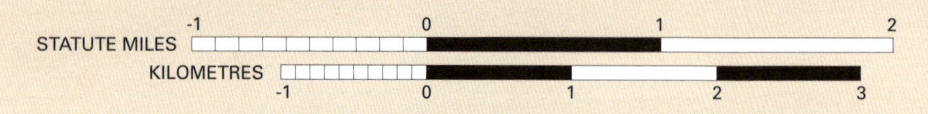

STATUTE MILES -1 0 1 2
KILOMETRES -1 0 1 2 3

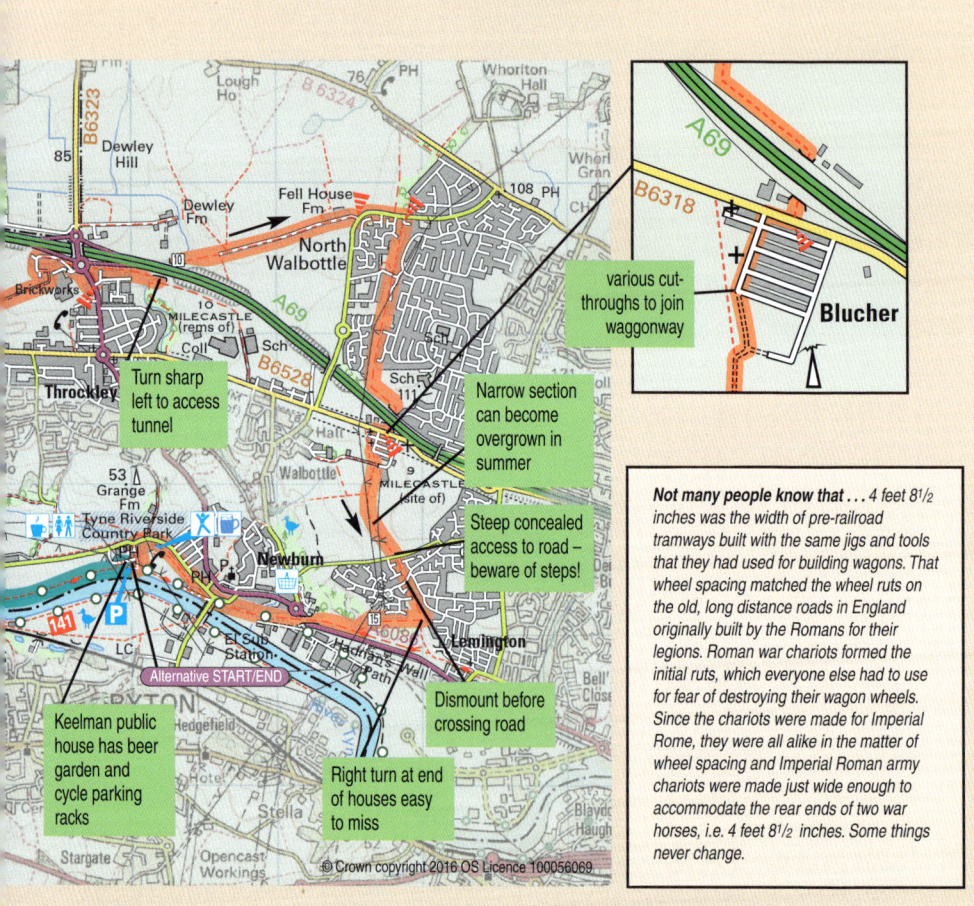

Turn sharp left to access tunnel

various cut-throughs to join waggonway

Narrow section can become overgrown in summer

Steep concealed access to road – beware of steps!

Dismount before crossing road

Right turn at end of houses easy to miss

Keelman public house has beer garden and cycle parking racks

Alternative START/END

© Crown copyright 2016 OS Licence 100056069

Not many people know that... 4 feet 8½ inches was the width of pre-railroad tramways built with the same jigs and tools that they had used for building wagons. That wheel spacing matched the wheel ruts on the old, long distance roads in England originally built by the Romans for their legions. Roman war chariots formed the initial ruts, which everyone else had to use for fear of destroying their wagon wheels. Since the chariots were made for Imperial Rome, they were all alike in the matter of wheel spacing and Imperial Roman army chariots were made just wide enough to accommodate the rear ends of two war horses, i.e. 4 feet 8½ inches. Some things never change.

Total distance	21.6 km
Total ascent /descent	230 metres

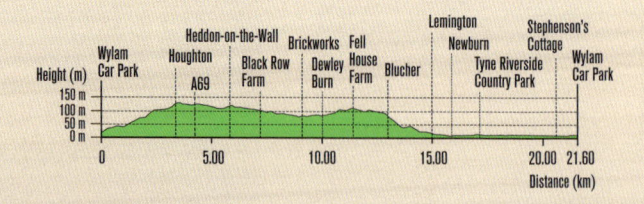

96

Waggonways & Bridleways 25

Riding the bridleway towards Donkins House Farm

Ponteland & Heddon-on-the-Wall Loop

DISTANCE: 28 km / 18 miles

GRADE: Moderate

START/END
Ponteland
FREE PARKING: car park next to the B6323 near to the fire station

Ordnance Survey maps:
Explorer 316 – Newcastle-upon-Tyne
Landranger 88 – Newcastle-upon-Tyne

SUMMARY: This loop cleverly links semi-urban tracts to the west of Newcastle with residential and rural fringe areas. Essentially bi-directional, cycling clockwise just edges it to benefit from several slight gradients you will encounter.

Assuming a Ponteland start, the route begins with almost 2 km of shared-use rail path which closely but safely passes the Newcastle airport roundabout to join the Low Luddick bridleway. This section provides a unique end-of-runway view of Newcastle airport. It is then necessary to negotiate two mini-roundabouts on the A696 flyover to access the B6918 which has a shared-use path on its east side linking to a narrow cycle lane. Turn first right then first left along a quiet residential street at the end of which you need to turn right to access and carefully cross the Metro line at an approved crossing point. After 200 m, turn right to follow a wide bridleway to near Butterslaw. Note that the first 40 m can be muddy after rain. The route via Heddon-on-the-Wall to Eachwick and the west end of Darras Hall Estate is easy to map-read and follow from here and then you rejoin the popular, shared-use rail path back to the starting point. Look out for the sharp right turn after the anti-motorbike access control close to Ponteland.

Not many people know that . . . the Ponteland and Darras Hall Branch railway opened in 1905 was an 11 km (6.8 miles) single-track branch railway line that ran from South Gosforth to Ponteland past a sub-line to Darras Hall. The line closed to passengers on the 17th June 1929 but stayed open for freight. Parts of the line were taken over in stages to become part of the Tyne-&-Wear Metro.

ROUTE NOTES:

This route crosses a number of residential roads and a few main roads, all of which need care.

(1) **TAKE EXTRA CARE** when negotiating the two mini-roundabouts and crossing the Metro line at Callerton Parkway Station.

(2) **TAKE EXTRA CARE** when crossing the road link between Woolsington and Low Luddick.

(3) The B6918 road to / from Ponteland can be busy at times.

(4) **TAKE EXTRA CARE** when crossing the main road north of Throckley.

LOOS & BREWS:

Heddon-on-the-Wall: The Three Tuns Inn – cyclists welcome, The White Swan; and a tea-room (slightly off route) garage shop / WC
Callerton: The Wheatsheaf – 01912 869254
Ponteland: The Diamond Inn (slightly off route)

97

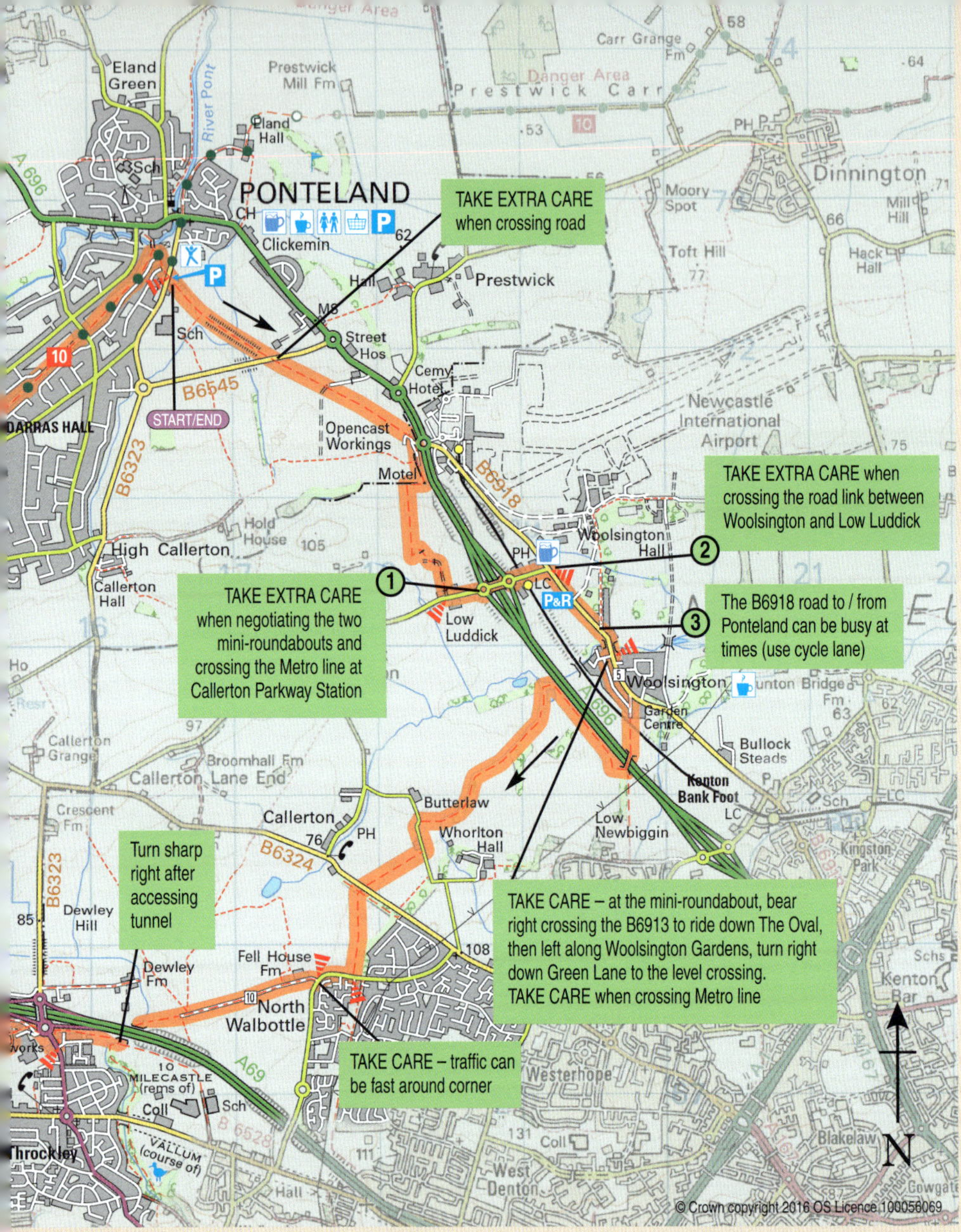

PONTELAND
TAKE EXTRA CARE when crossing road
START/END
DARRAS HALL
TAKE EXTRA CARE when crossing the road link between Woolsington and Low Luddick
TAKE EXTRA CARE when negotiating the two mini-roundabouts and crossing the Metro line at Callerton Parkway Station
The B6918 road to / from Ponteland can be busy at times (use cycle lane)
Turn sharp right after accessing tunnel
TAKE CARE – at the mini-roundabout, bear right crossing the B6913 to ride down The Oval, then left along Woolsington Gardens, turn right down Green Lane to the level crossing.
TAKE CARE when crossing Metro line
TAKE CARE – traffic can be fast around corner
Newcastle International Airport
Woolsington
Low Luddick
High Callerton
Callerton
Butterlaw
Whorlton Hall
Fell House Fm
North Walbottle
Throckley
Prestwick
Dinnington
Kenton Bank Foot
Westerhope
West Denton
B6545
B6323
B6918
B6324
A696
A69
N

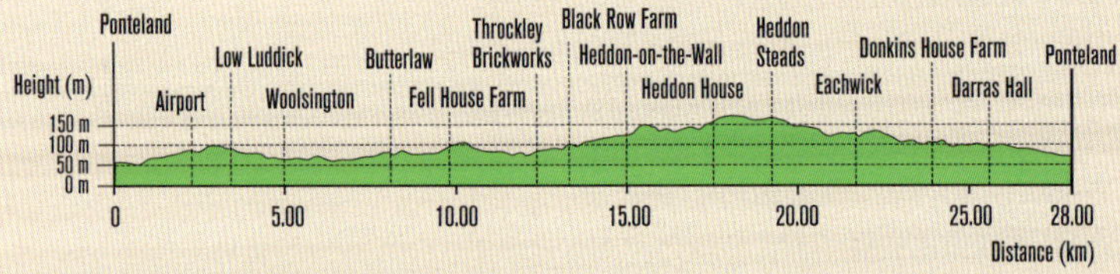

Ponteland
Airport
Low Luddick
Woolsington
Butterlaw
Fell House Farm
Throckley Brickworks
Black Row Farm
Heddon-on-the-Wall
Heddon House
Heddon Steads
Eachwick
Donkins House Farm
Darras Hall
Ponteland
Height (m)
150 m
100 m
50 m
0 m
0
5.00
10.00
15.00
20.00
25.00
28.00
Distance (km)

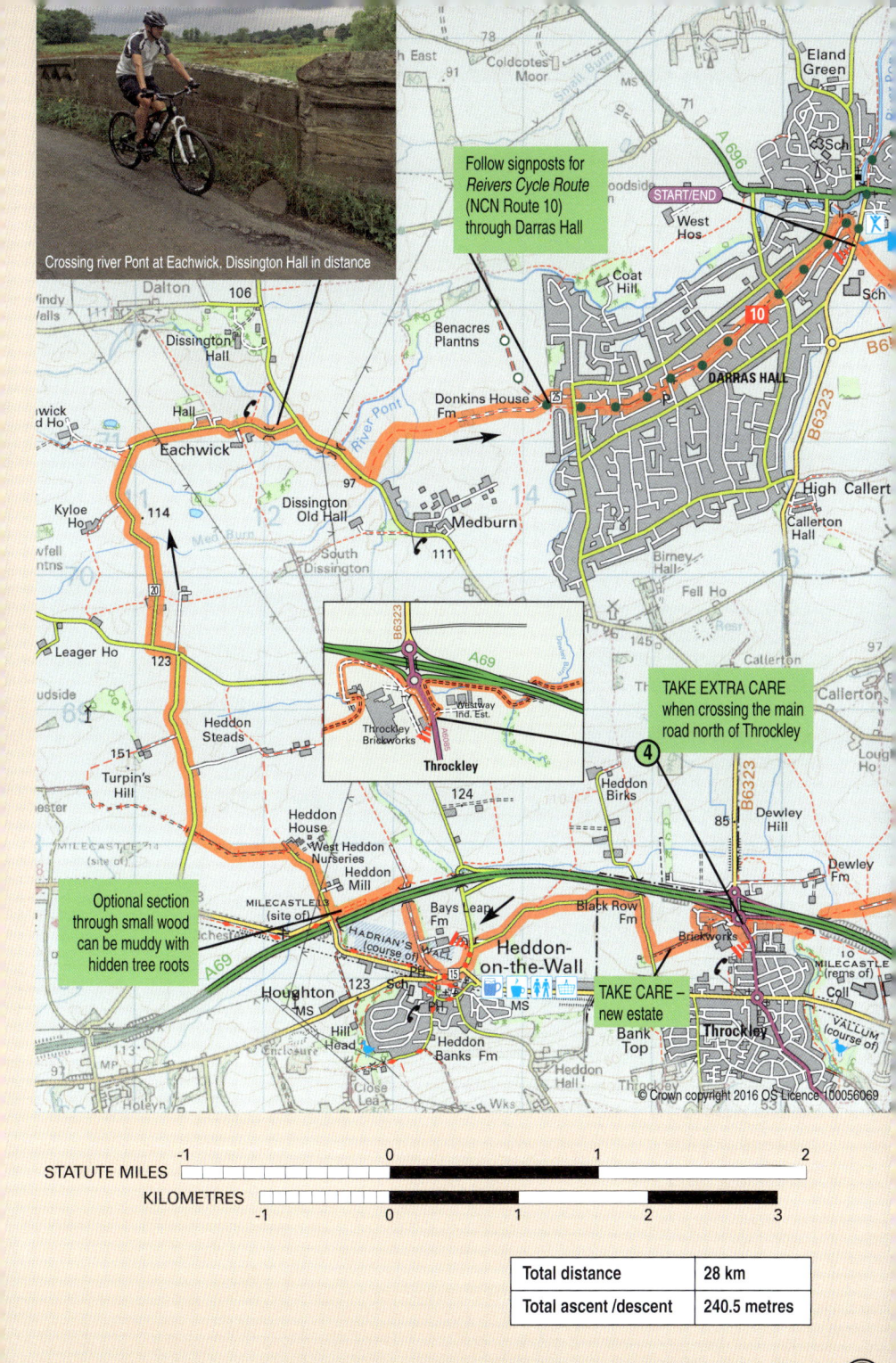

Crossing river Pont at Eachwick, Dissington Hall in distance

Follow signposts for *Reivers Cycle Route* (NCN Route 10) through Darras Hall

TAKE EXTRA CARE when crossing the main road north of Throckley

Optional section through small wood can be muddy with hidden tree roots

TAKE CARE – new estate

Total distance	28 km
Total ascent /descent	240.5 metres

99

Waggonways & Bridleways 26

On the well-maintained Waggonway between North Walbottle and Callerton

Throckley Dene & Woolsington Figure of Eight

DISTANCE: 16.4 km / 10 miles

GRADE: Moderate

START/END
Newburn
Tyne Riverside Country Park
FREE PARKING: Newburn – Tyne Riverside Country Park

Ordnance Survey maps:
Explorer 316 – Newcastle-upon-Tyne
Landranger 88 – Newcastle-upon-Tyne

SUMMARY: The very pleasant bi-directional *Throckley Dene & Woolsington Figure of Eight* is one of the shorter routes in this guide with an enjoyable, gravity-assisted descent to the riverside whichever way the lower part of this route is ridden. The downside of this is the upside, i.e. the uphill return route to North Walbottle. If this part of the route is done anticlockwise, only 400 m of the lower third of the Lemington option is quite steep to cycle up but it's not far to push. If the bottom half of the loop is ridden clockwise, then there are two short pushes for all but the very fit – one up to Grange Farm and the approach up to the B6528. Throckley Dene is an adventurous scenic cycle ride at any time of the year. At the time of publication, the Whorlton Hall link is as shown on the map insert and is well-used by the public. It too will be muddy in places after rain, so pushing your bike is recommended until a better short link is created as part of a new housing development. The figure of eight shapes provides two looplets.

ROUTE NOTES:

① Be traffic-aware when crossing the B6528 twice and the B6324 – use the verge path for this section but give way to pedestrians.

② Throckley Dene does become slippery after rain but it's lovely to cycle when it's dry.

LOOS & BREWS:
Newburn: Keelman public house – 0191 267 0772
The Boathouse – 0191 229 0326; nearby shops
Newburn Activity Centre: offers bike hire for individuals and groups
Heddon-on-the-Wall: two public houses and a tea-room (slightly off route)

Not many people know that ... historically, Newburn was larger than Newcastle-upon-Tyne as it was the eastern most fordable point of the River Tyne so had strong Roman links along with Walbottle. The name Walbottle dates back to 1176 as "Walbotl" which is derived from the Old English 'botl' meaning 'building on the Roman Wall'. Both villages transformed with the Industrial Revolution, when large collieries and a steelworks opened but these industries declined and Newburn is now home to a country park and various leisure facilities.

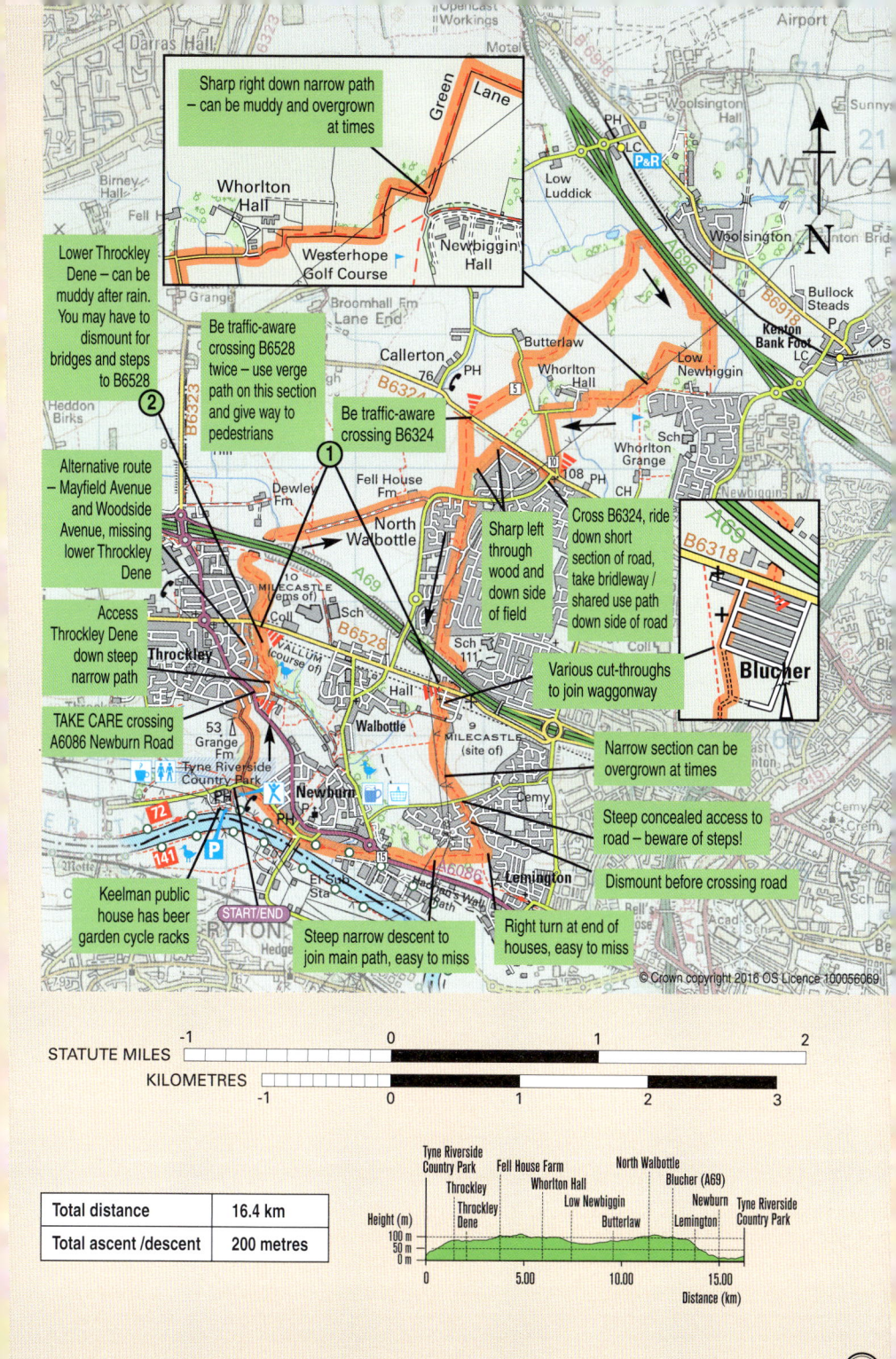

Total distance	16.4 km
Total ascent /descent	200 metres

Waggonways & Bridleways 27

Family-friendly section of waggonway, High Weetslade

Newcastle & North Tyneside Loop

DISTANCE: 27 km / 17 miles

GRADE: Moderate

Family-friendly section

START/END
Wallsend
Rising Sun Country Park
FREE PARKING: Rising Sun Country Park

Alternative START/END
Hazlerigg – FREE PARKING:
Coach Lane car park and picnic area / Havannah Nature Reserve

INFORMATION
www.visitnorthtyneside.com

Ordnance Survey maps:

Explorer 316 – Newcastle-upon-Tyne

Landranger 88 – Newcastle-upon-Tyne

SUMMARY: *The Newcastle & North Tyneside Waggonways Loop* is a celebration of off-road, semi-urban cycling at its best, linked by some relatively quiet residential streets. Undoubtedly, our mining heritage is the key to making this route possible as it uses waggonways aplenty and takes fullest advantage of the legacy of the Rising Sun pit site, now an excellent country park. The whole route is an enjoyable cycling journey of discovery and whilst this guide isn't the right place to recount north-east mining history, it provides the opportunity for cyclists to enjoy pedalling some of its leftovers which are now community assets. Use the more detailed inset maps to aid your navigation to cycle this bi-directional at the more tricky locations. Undoubtedly, navigating as shown on the map between Longbenton and Holystone will need your full attention for the first of many times you will cycle this route. Do stop to read the many en-route information panels. The views from the top of the Rising Sun hill and the hill at Weetslade are well worth the extra effort.

ROUTE NOTES:
all main road crossing points are light-controlled or use under-bridges. New housing has significantly changed the area around Holystone Farm.

LOOS & BREWS:
Wallsend: Rising Sun Country Park Visitor Centre, café / WC
NE12 9SS – 0191 643 2241

Holystone: The Holystone – 0191 266 6173

Not many people know that... The Rising Sun colliery was one of the largest in Europe with circa 60 miles of tunnels. The colliery first produced coal in 1908 and there was always the danger of an explosion as the coal was gassy and sulphurous. By 1931 it employed 2,000 men and in 1961 produced 475,871 tonnes of coal. The pit finally closed in 1969 with the discovery of natural gas, putting 1,180 men and 26 pit ponies out of work. The 400-acre Rising Sun site is now a Green Flag award-winning country park with a visitor centre and an organic farm with woodland and wetland habitats teeming with wildlife.

102

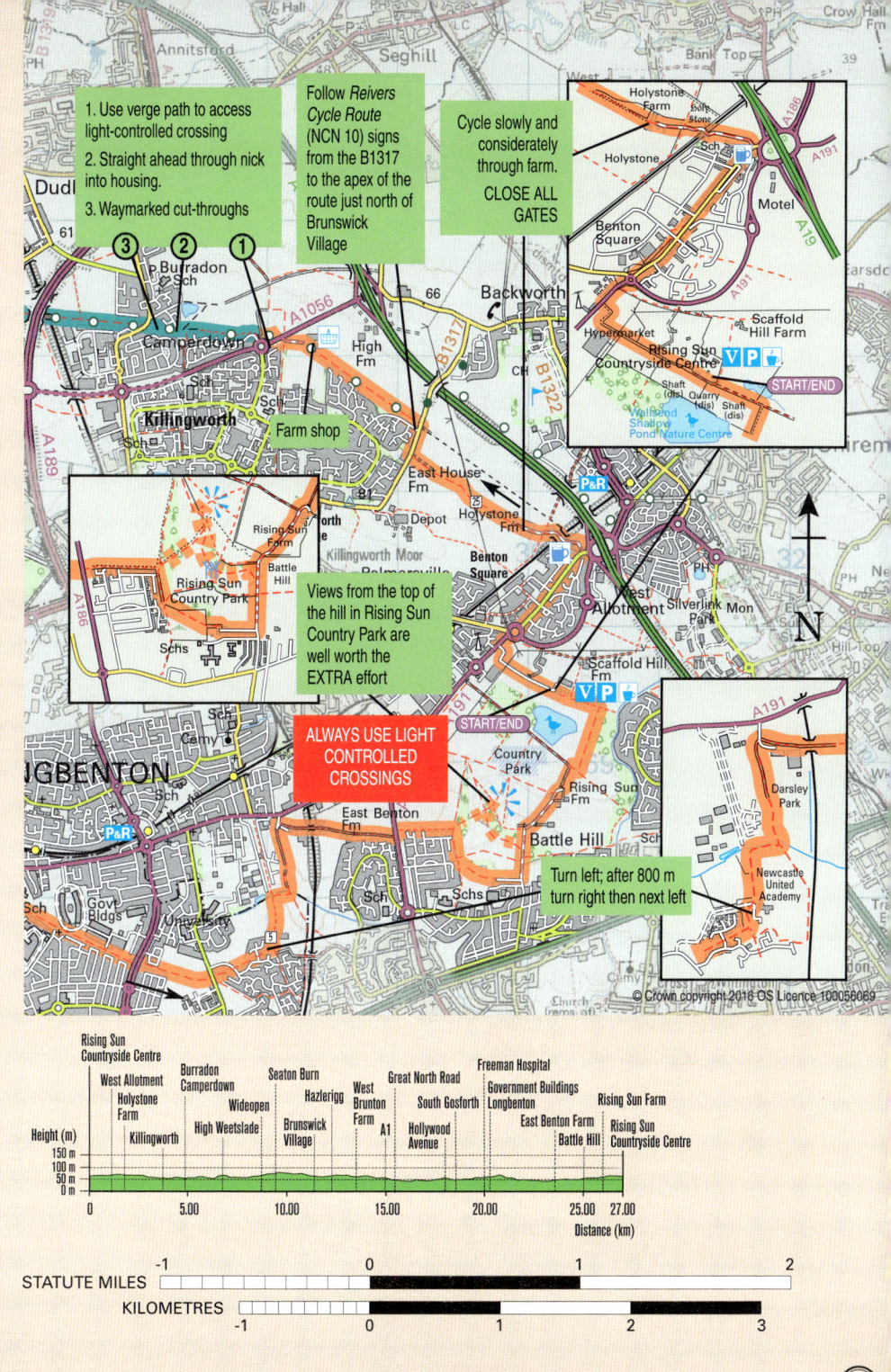

1. Use verge path to access light-controlled crossing
2. Straight ahead through nick into housing.
3. Waymarked cut-throughs

Follow *Reivers Cycle Route* (NCN 10) signs from the B1317 to the apex of the route just north of Brunswick Village

Cycle slowly and considerately through farm.
CLOSE ALL GATES

Farm shop

Views from the top of the hill in Rising Sun Country Park are well worth the EXTRA effort

ALWAYS USE LIGHT CONTROLLED CROSSINGS

Turn left; after 800 m turn right then next left

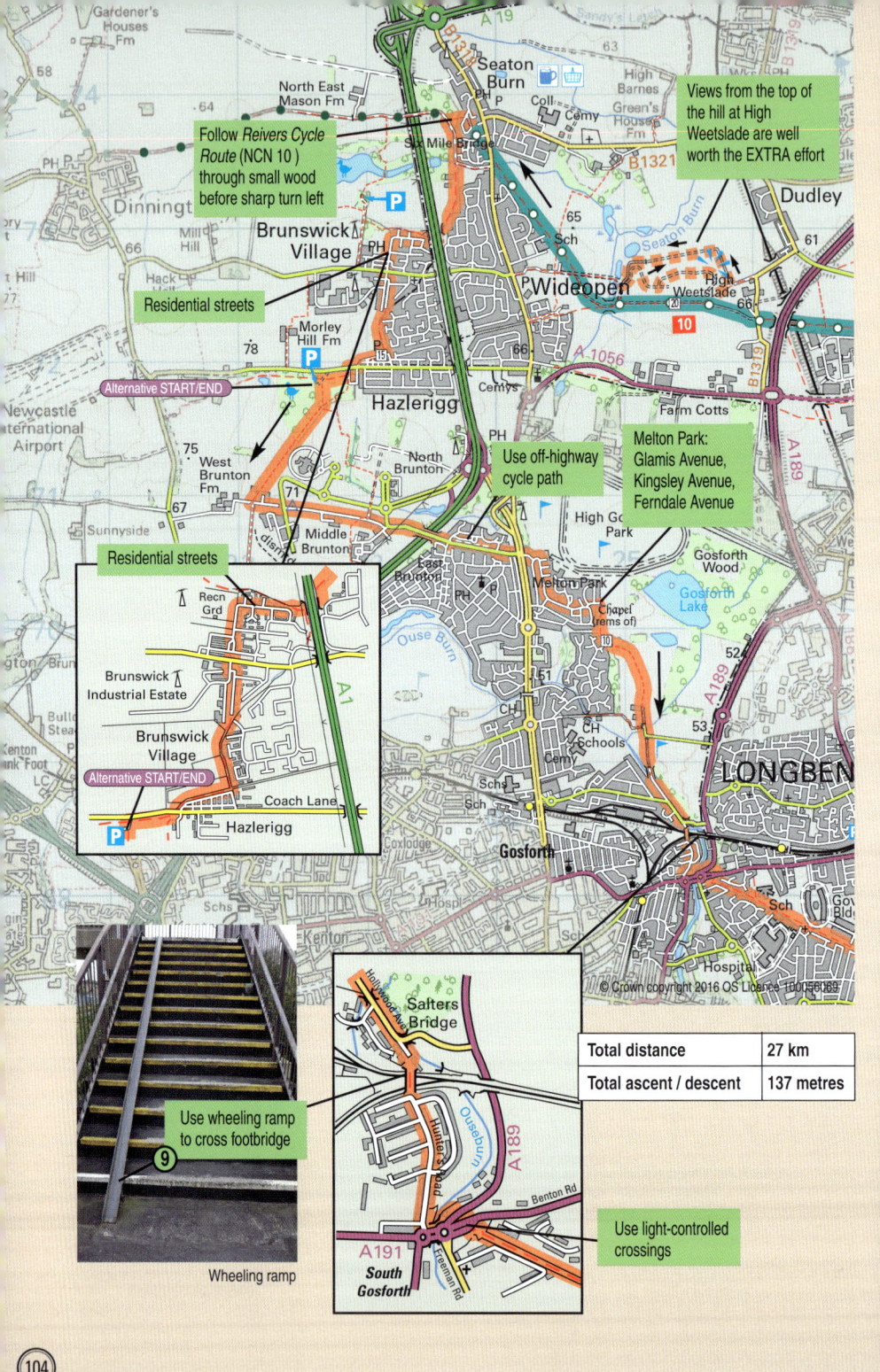

Follow *Reivers Cycle Route* (NCN 10) through small wood before sharp turn left

Views from the top of the hill at High Weetslade are well worth the EXTRA effort

Residential streets

Alternative START/END

Use off-highway cycle path

Melton Park: Glamis Avenue, Kingsley Avenue, Ferndale Avenue

Residential streets

Alternative START/END

Use wheeling ramp to cross footbridge

Wheeling ramp

Use light-controlled crossings

Total distance	27 km
Total ascent / descent	137 metres

104

Waggonways & Bridleways 28

Killingworth Lake

Killingworth & Gosforth Loop

DISTANCE: 23.4 km / 14.6 miles

GRADE: Easy

Family-friendly section

START/END
Killingworth
FREE PARKING: Northumberland Way car park close to Killingworth Lake.

Alternative START/END
Hazlerigg
Havannah Nature Reserve
FREE PARKING: Coach Lane car park and picnic area / Havannah Nature Reserve

SUMMARY: The bi-directional *Killingworth & Gosforth Loop* is a creative interweaving of a number of ex-mining communities not far to the north-east of Newcastle-upon-Tyne. Join it at any suitable point but be sure to follow the recommended route to cross main roads safely and avoid finding yourself on roads that aren't cycle-friendly. It's an enjoyable sortie so don't be put off by the route detail.

The route description assumes the eastern of the two starting points highlighted leading past the west end of Killingworth Lake. The inset map shows the route through houses up to Camperdown. Ascending to Weetslade view point and sculpture is worth the effort before re-joining Route 10 just east of Dinnington. Enjoy the tracks through Havannah Nature Reserve before crossing Brunton Lane down almost to the new houses at Fawdon, before turning left towards residential housing in Newcastle Great Park. Rejoin Brunton Lane and use the cycle lane to access the light-controlled crossing over the Great North Road. Follow the indicated residential streets through Melton Park to join a surprisingly rural lane leading to Gosforth golf course before turning left along Heathery Lane to the light-controlled crossing of Salter's Lane. Cycle paths lead around Balliol Business Park and after safely crossing Benton Road (A188), head north on a cycle path to West Moor. Take the second right along residential Westmoor Drive which leads to the railway under-bridge and Albert Terrace. After crossing Great Lime Road, it's a relatively short, cycle-friendly distance with open ground on your right to join Northumberland Way, where a left turn will bring you back to the start.

Ordnance Survey maps:
Explorer 316 – Newcastle-upon-Tyne
Landranger 88 – Newcastle-upon-Tyne

LOOS & BREWS:
numerous pubs en route

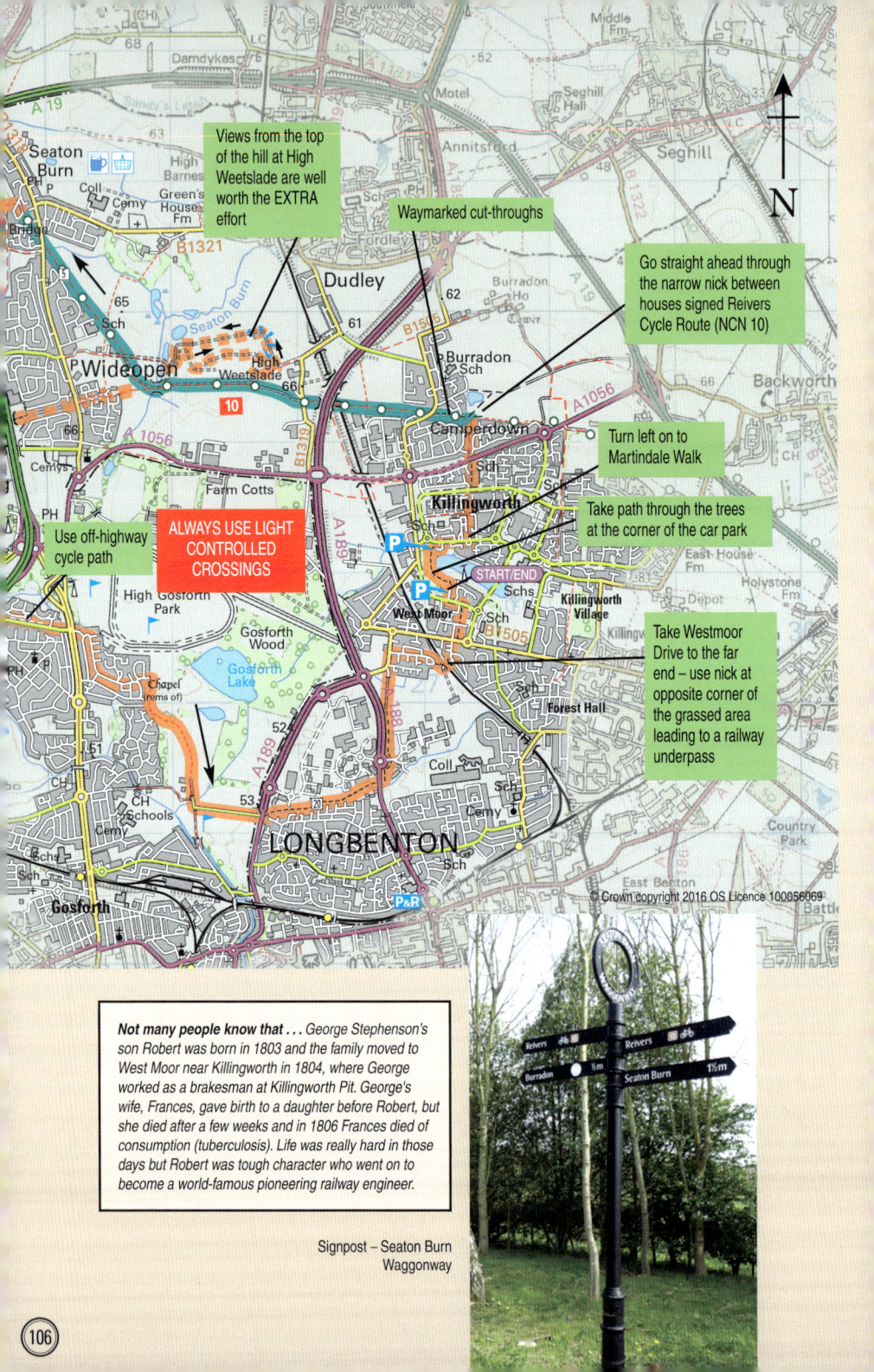

Views from the top of the hill at High Weetslade are well worth the EXTRA effort

Waymarked cut-throughs

Go straight ahead through the narrow nick between houses signed Reivers Cycle Route (NCN 10)

Turn left on to Martindale Walk

Take path through the trees at the corner of the car park

ALWAYS USE LIGHT CONTROLLED CROSSINGS

Use off-highway cycle path

Take Westmoor Drive to the far end – use nick at opposite corner of the grassed area leading to a railway underpass

Not many people know that . . . George Stephenson's son Robert was born in 1803 and the family moved to West Moor near Killingworth in 1804, where George worked as a brakesman at Killingworth Pit. George's wife, Frances, gave birth to a daughter before Robert, but she died after a few weeks and in 1806 Frances died of consumption (tuberculosis). Life was really hard in those days but Robert was tough character who went on to become a world-famous pioneering railway engineer.

Signpost – Seaton Burn Waggonway

106

Path bypasses Hack Hall

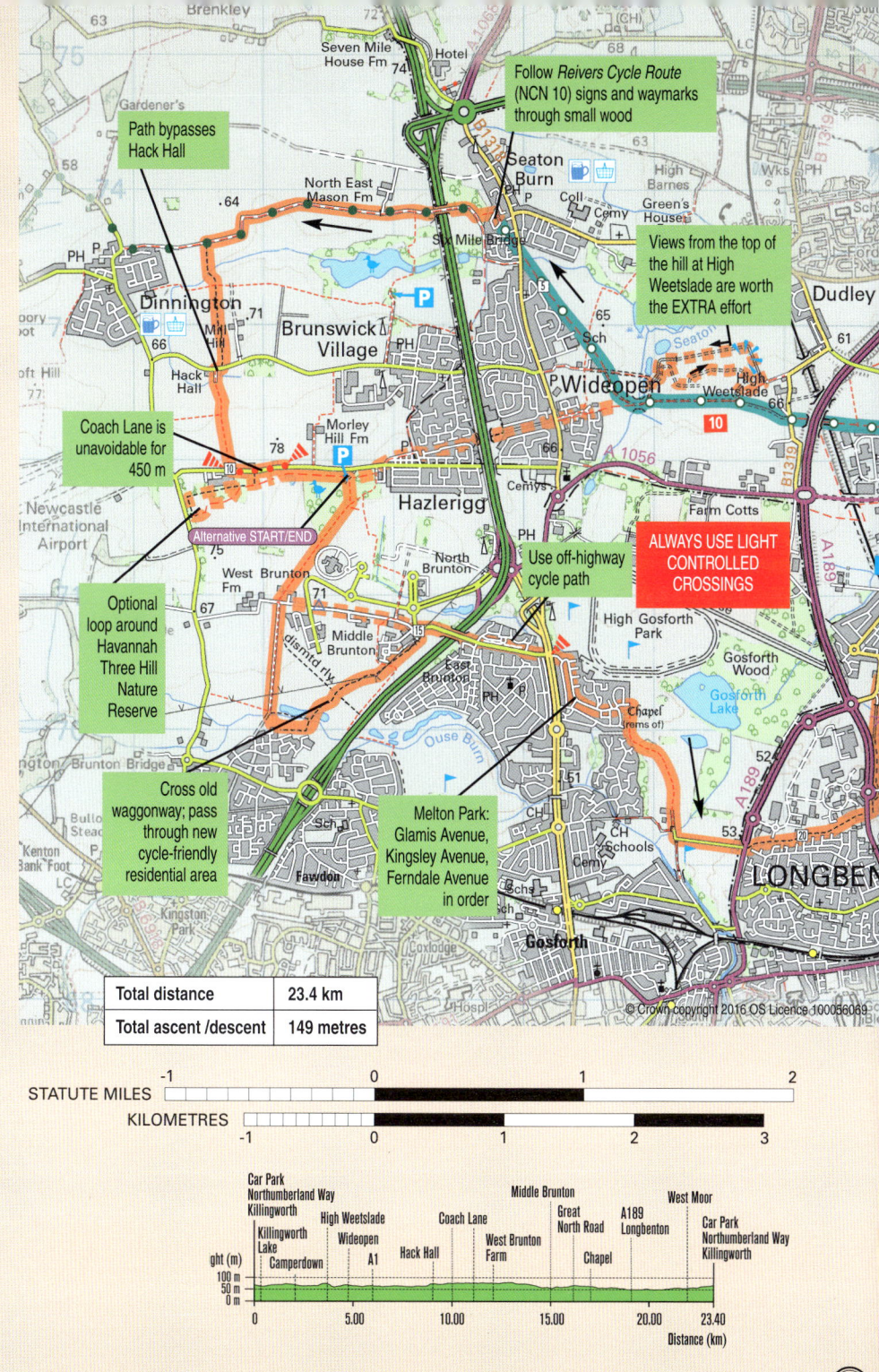

Follow *Reivers Cycle Route* (NCN 10) signs and waymarks through small wood

Views from the top of the hill at High Weetslade are worth the EXTRA effort

Coach Lane is unavoidable for 450 m

Use off-highway cycle path

ALWAYS USE LIGHT CONTROLLED CROSSINGS

Optional loop around Havannah Three Hill Nature Reserve

Cross old waggonway; pass through new cycle-friendly residential area

Melton Park: Glamis Avenue, Kingsley Avenue, Ferndale Avenue in order

Total distance	23.4 km
Total ascent /descent	149 metres

© Crown copyright 2016 OS Licence 100056089

107

Waggonways & Bridleways 29

Family-friendly section of waggonway between Backworth and Seghill

Cramlington & Backworth Loop

DISTANCE: 31.75 km / 20 miles

GRADE: Easy

START/END
Backworth
FREE PARKING: corner of Church Road

Family-friendly sections

Alternative START/END
Brenkley Road:
FREE PARKING: Brenkley Road (NB: The opencast is now re-landscaped)

SUMMARY: *The Cramlington & Backworth Loop* follows numerous waggonways, a few bridleways, several purpose-built cycle paths, an old car-free road and sections of minor road. Main roads are crossed either using light-controlled crossings or underpasses. The loop can be ridden in either direction but anticlockwise is recommended as the left turn adjacent to the A1068 north of Seaton Burn, and again on to and along the short section of C road north of Dinnington, is more cycle-friendly in that direction.

Backworth is the eastern of the two identified start points. It is very close to the Backworth Waggonway which leads to Seghill and on to Cramlington, and the loop via Middle Farm bypasses a difficult section. After passing under the A189, the waggonway becomes a 4-metre wide cycleway through Cramlington until the route curves north at the park and grass triangle. After turning left at the church and passing under the A117 and crossing the railway, the route enters more rural terrain before joining Arcot Road which leads to the light-controlled crossing of the large A19 roundabout. Take the shortcut or be more adventurous and extend the loop via Dinnington to join the *Reivers Cycle Route* (NCN Route10). After Camperdown the route is fairly straightforward to the east of Holystone Farm, where new housing is changing the landscape. A protected bridleway links to an on-going, gravel cycle path. Cross the B1322 at the light-controlled crossing, continue east before turning sharp right under the duelled road, down the side of the railway track to the railway crossing point, to then cycle up the other side passing under the flyover before curving right then left back to the start.

Ordnance Survey maps:

Explorer 316 – Newcastle-upon-Tyne

Landranger 88 – Newcastle-upon-Tyne

ROUTE NOTES:

All main roads are crossed using light-controlled crossings or underpasses.

① **TAKE EXTRA CARE** when linking Arcot Road with the cycle path adjacent to the A1068.

② Optional shortcut through Seaton Burn, using the sometimes busy B1318 for 700 metres.

LOOS & BREWS: numerous pubs en route

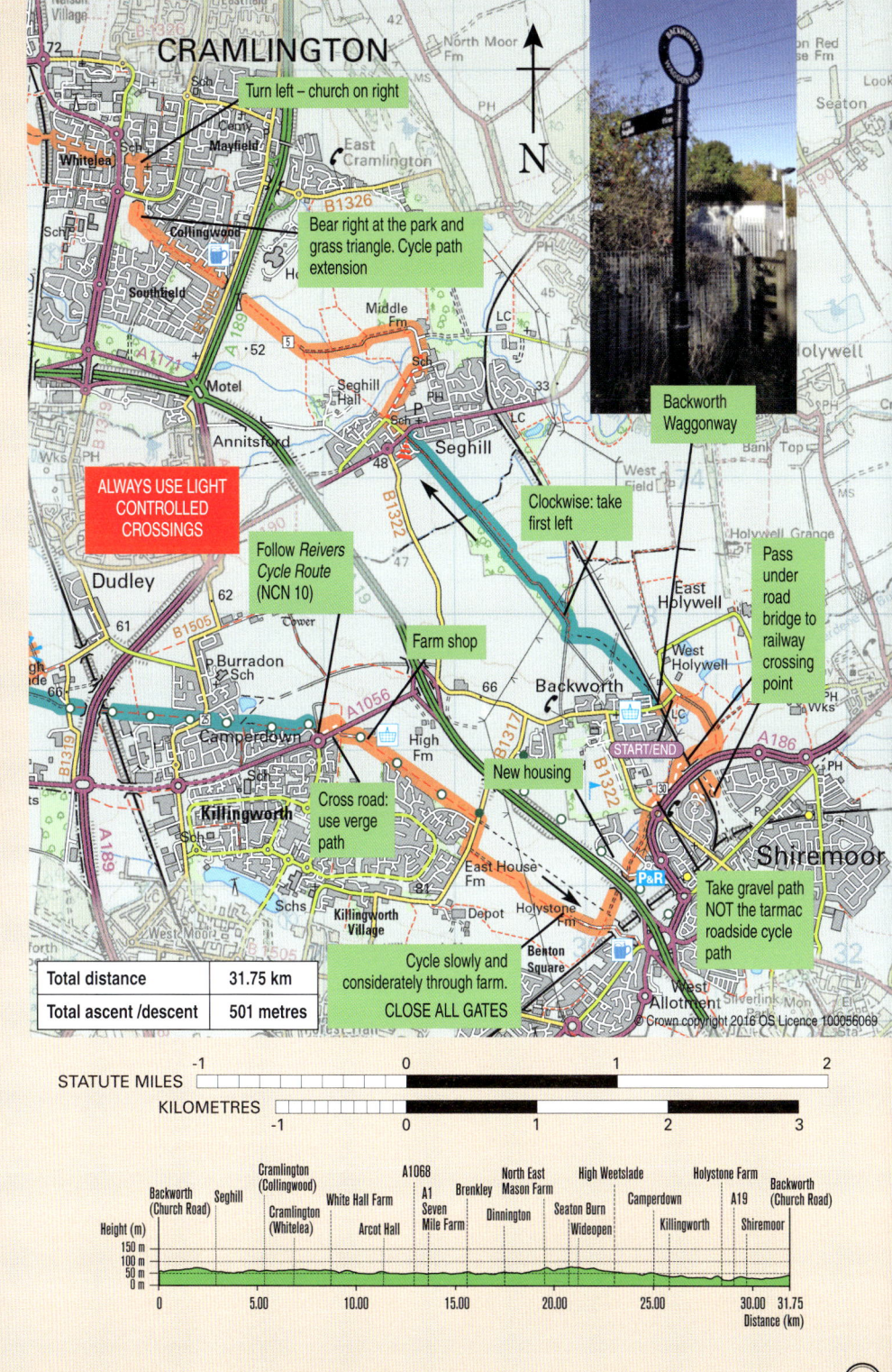

CRAMLINGTON

- Turn left – church on right
- Bear right at the park and grass triangle. Cycle path extension
- ALWAYS USE LIGHT CONTROLLED CROSSINGS
- Follow *Reivers Cycle Route* (NCN 10)
- Farm shop
- Cross road: use verge path
- Cycle slowly and considerately through farm. CLOSE ALL GATES
- Clockwise: take first left
- New housing
- Backworth Waggonway
- Pass under road bridge to railway crossing point
- Take gravel path NOT the tarmac roadside cycle path

| Total distance | 31.75 km |
| Total ascent /descent | 501 metres |

© Crown copyright 2016 OS Licence 100056069

STATUTE MILES: -1, 0, 1, 2
KILOMETRES: -1, 0, 1, 2, 3

Height (m): 150 m, 100 m, 50 m, 0 m
Distance (km): 0, 5.00, 10.00, 15.00, 20.00, 25.00, 30.00, 31.75

Backworth (Church Road) — Seghill — Cramlington (Collingwood) — Cramlington (Whitelea) — White Hall Farm — Arcot Hall — A1068 Seven Mile Farm — Brenkley — North East Mason Farm — Dinnington — High Weetslade — Seaton Burn Wideopen — Camperdown — Killingworth — Holystone Farm — A19 — Shiremoor — Backworth (Church Road)

109

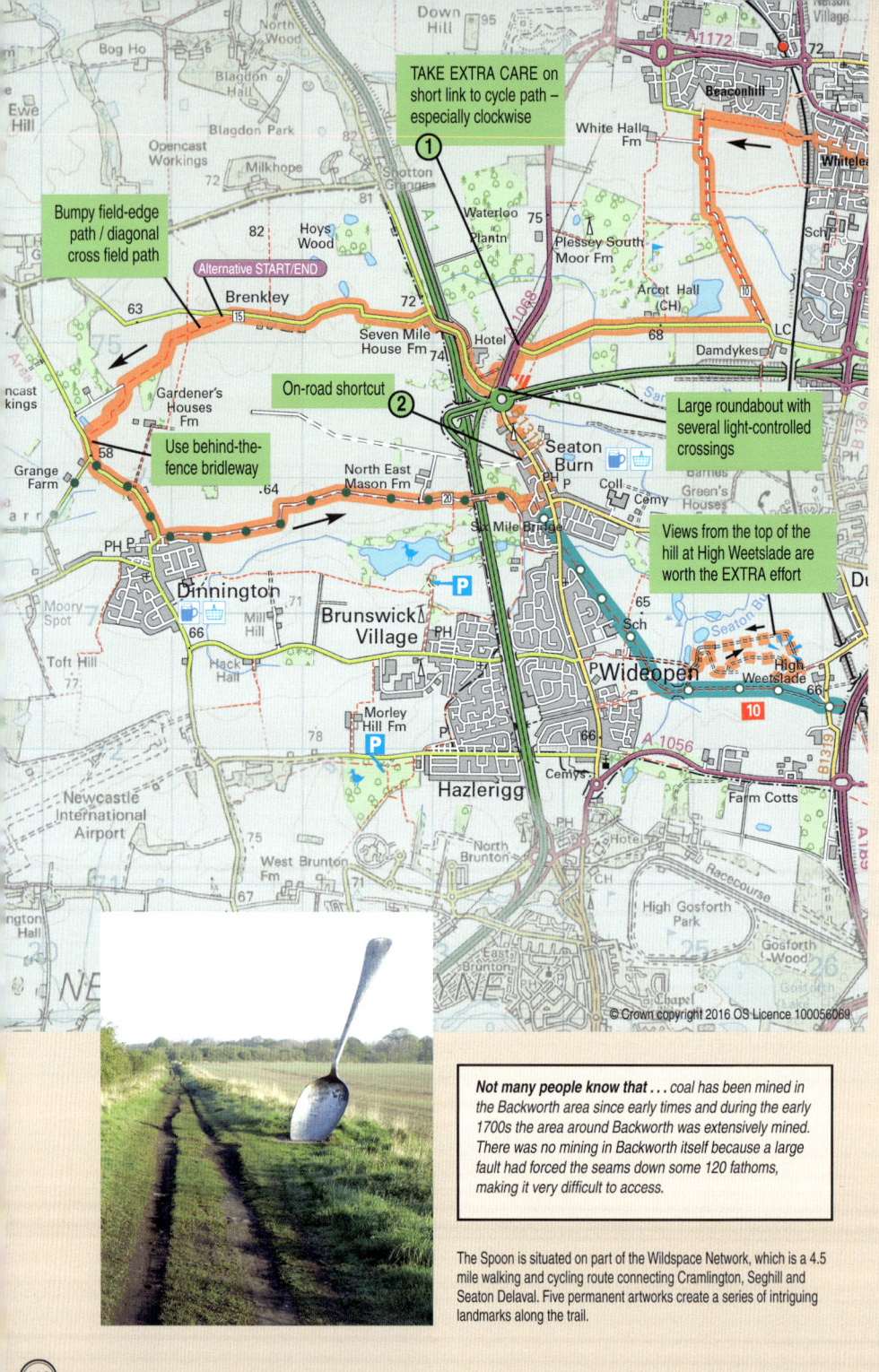

TAKE EXTRA CARE on short link to cycle path – especially clockwise

①

Bumpy field-edge path / diagonal cross field path

Alternative START/END

On-road shortcut

②

Use behind-the-fence bridleway

Large roundabout with several light-controlled crossings

Views from the top of the hill at High Weetslade are worth the EXTRA effort

© Crown copyright 2016 OS Licence 100056069

Not many people know that... coal has been mined in the Backworth area since early times and during the early 1700s the area around Backworth was extensively mined. There was no mining in Backworth itself because a large fault had forced the seams down some 120 fathoms, making it very difficult to access.

The Spoon is situated on part of the Wildspace Network, which is a 4.5 mile walking and cycling route connecting Cramlington, Seghill and Seaton Delaval. Five permanent artworks create a series of intriguing landmarks along the trail.

Waggonways & Bridleways 30

On the cliff-top path near Old Hartley

Tynemouth, Coast & Inland Loop

DISTANCE: 25.75 km / 16 miles **GRADE: Easy**

Family-friendly sections

SUMMARY: *The Tynemouth, Coast & Inland Waggonways Loop* is probably the one route in this compendium that comprises the most contrasting component sections. The mix includes a sea-front highway, promenades, cycle paths, a cliff-top Greenway, a heart of the countryside bridleway (Holywell Dene), farm access tracks, old waggonways and a fish quay. Scenery includes the mouth of a major UK river, the first lifeboat station in the world, an old priory and castle, sandy beaches, Cullercoats harbour, the Spanish City, St Mary's lighthouse, the High and Low level lights at North Shields, the Black Middens and Collingwood's Monument. The loop is bi-directional, but anticlockwise is the best option if only to free-wheel from Old Hartley to the start of Holywell Dene and that's the best way to cycle through Holywell village. Follow Route 10 signs from just south of the A186 underpass before joining *Hadrian's Cycleway* (NCN Route 72) at the Royal Quays.

ROUTE NOTES:

Take extra care whilst cycling the road sections – along the sea front, Old Hartley to the start of Holywell Dene, through Holywell Village and around the Fish Quay area.

Part of route 31 provides a shorter version of this route via Briar Dene.

① Anticlockwise – turn right down Watts Slope to access the promenade opposite the Spanish City.

② After a short, shared-walkway section, turn left down a steep slope by old steps to cross a footbridge; turn right, then after 100 m the path follows the field edge.

③ Take the underpass under the A186 to join the *Reivers Cycle Route* (NCN Route 10)

LOOS & BREWS: numerous en route

START/END
Royal Quays
FREE PARKING: Royal Quays outlet. (Walk bicycle across crossing on dual carriageway to start route)

Alternative START/END
Numerous car parks between Tynemouth and St Mary's Lighthouse: fees apply

VISITOR INFORMATION
www.visitnorthtyneside.com
History of North Tyneside:
www.northtyneside.gov.uk

Ordnance Survey maps:
Explorer 316 – Newcastle-upon-Tyne
Landranger 88 – Newcastle-upon-Tyne

TAKE CARE westbound: crossing traffic flow

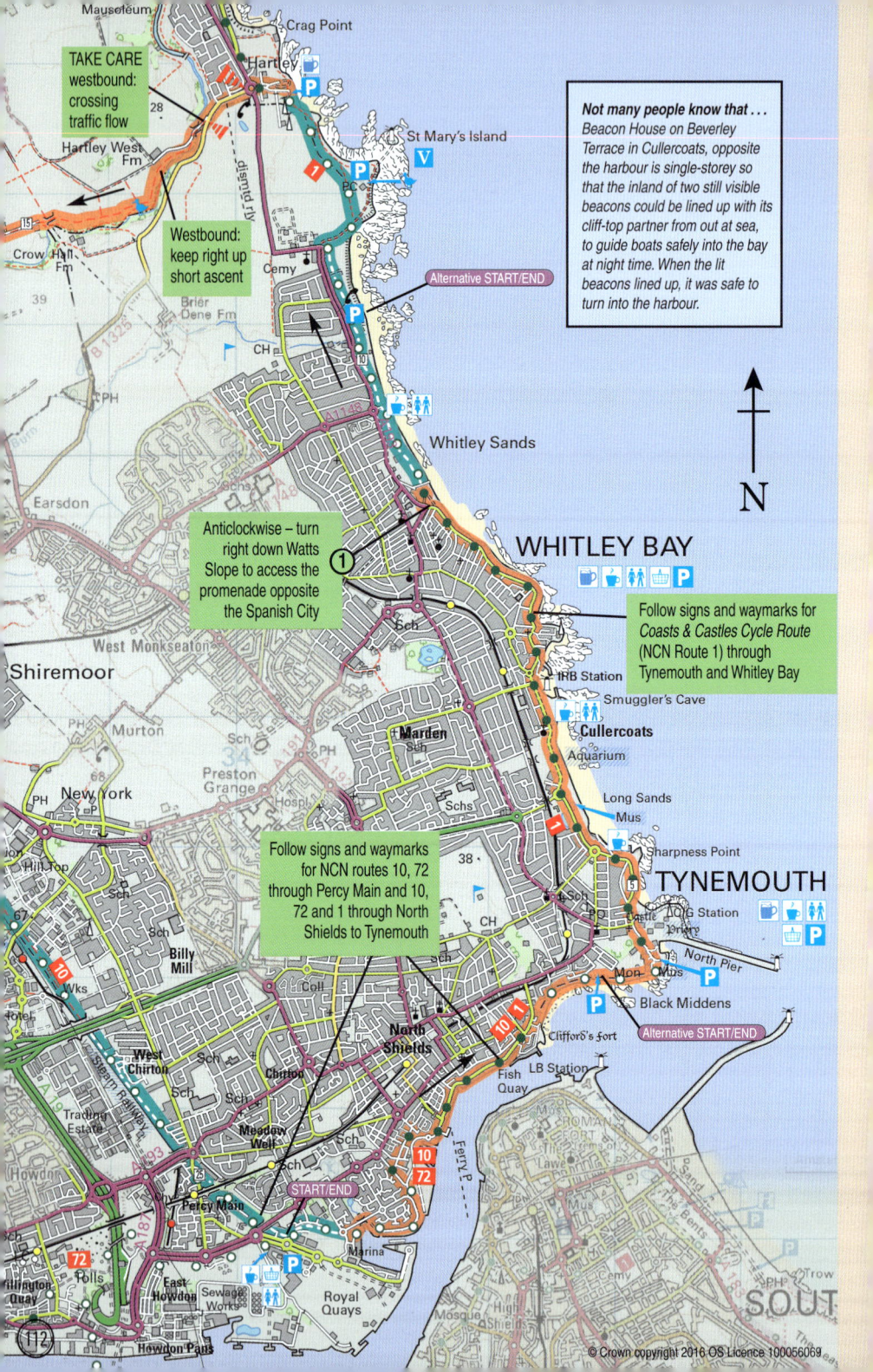

Westbound: keep right up short ascent

Not many people know that...
Beacon House on Beverley Terrace in Cullercoats, opposite the harbour is single-storey so that the inland of two still visible beacons could be lined up with its cliff-top partner from out at sea, to guide boats safely into the bay at night time. When the lit beacons lined up, it was safe to turn into the harbour.

Alternative START/END

N

Anticlockwise – turn right down Watts Slope to access the promenade opposite the Spanish City

WHITLEY BAY

Follow signs and waymarks for *Coasts & Castles Cycle Route* (NCN Route 1) through Tynemouth and Whitley Bay

TYNEMOUTH

Follow signs and waymarks for NCN routes 10, 72 through Percy Main and 10, 72 and 1 through North Shields to Tynemouth

Alternative START/END

START/END

© Crown copyright 2016 OS Licence 100056069

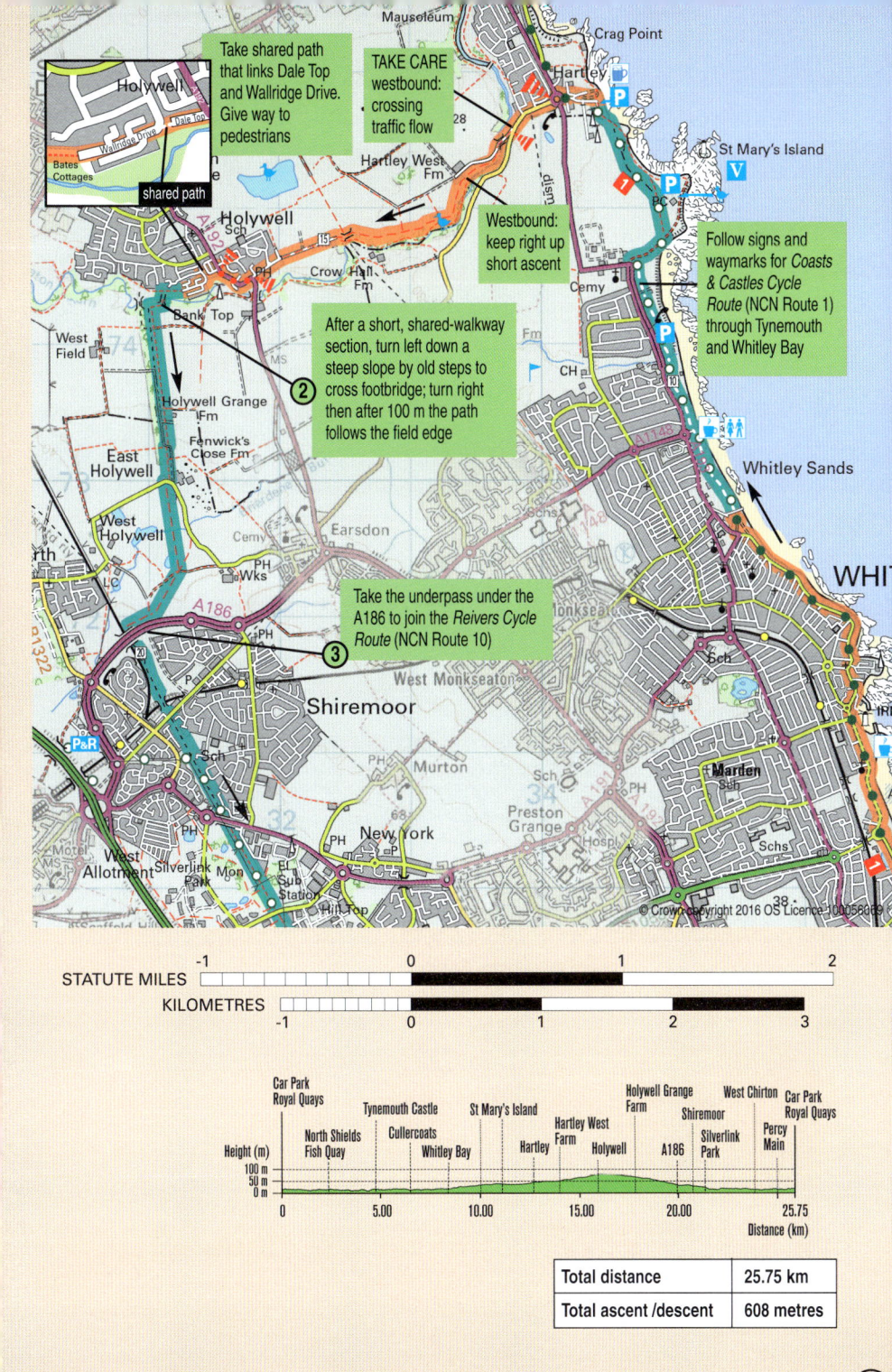

Take shared path that links Dale Top and Wallridge Drive. Give way to pedestrians

TAKE CARE westbound: crossing traffic flow

Westbound: keep right up short ascent

Follow signs and waymarks for *Coasts & Castles Cycle Route* (NCN Route 1) through Tynemouth and Whitley Bay

After a short, shared-walkway section, turn left down a steep slope by old steps to cross footbridge; turn right then after 100 m the path follows the field edge

Take the underpass under the A186 to join the *Reivers Cycle Route* (NCN Route 10)

Total distance	25.75 km
Total ascent /descent	608 metres

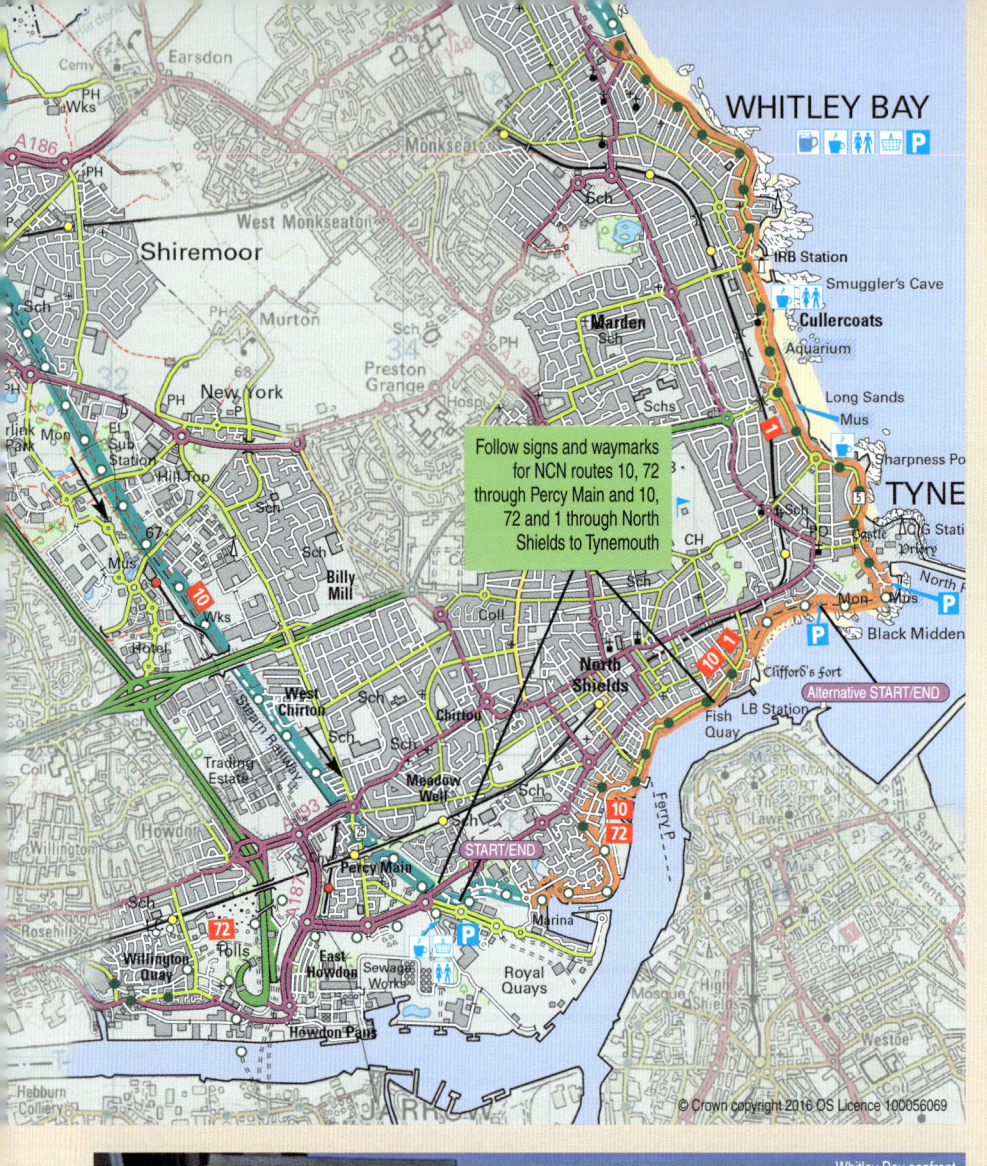

WHITLEY BAY

Follow signs and waymarks for NCN routes 10, 72 through Percy Main and 10, 72 and 1 through North Shields to Tynemouth

Whitley Bay seafront

114

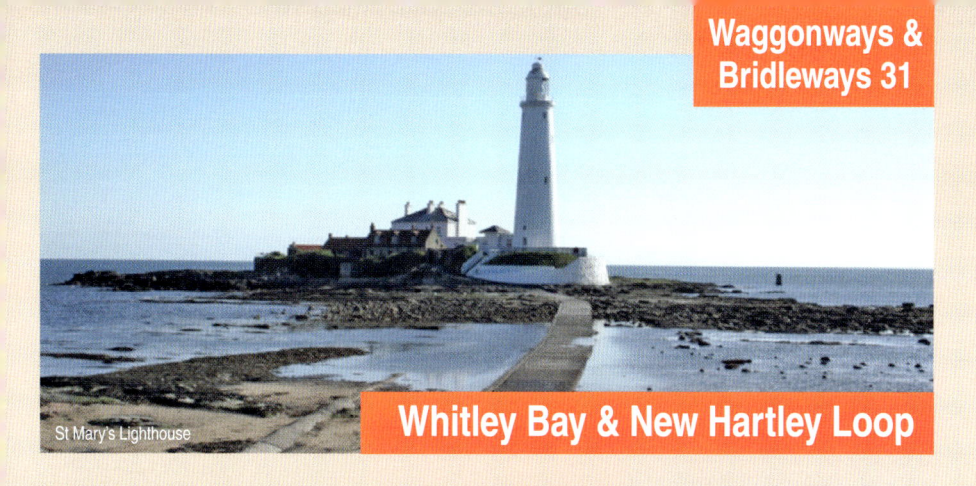

Waggonways & Bridleways 31

St Mary's Lighthouse

Whitley Bay & New Hartley Loop

DISTANCE: 16.7 km / 10.5 miles

Family-friendly sections

GRADE: Easy

START/END
Seaton Sluice
FREE PARKING: Seaton Sluice, Fountain Head car park

Alternative START/END
Whitley Bay, Briardene
PARKING: Briardene, The Links car park – fees apply

VISITOR INFORMATION
www.visitnorthtyneside.com
History of North Tyneside:
www.northtyneside.gov.uk

Ordnance Survey maps:
Explorer 316 – Newcastle-upon-Tyne
Landranger 88 – Newcastle-upon-Tyne

SUMMARY: Whilst the *Whitley Bay & New Hartley Loop* is a bi-directional route, anticlockwise is recommended for no other reason than the route through Whitley Bay flows better in this direction and is safer because there are no cross-flow turnings. This loop extends Route 30 northwards towards Blyth passing Charlie's Garden in Collywell Bay, Rocky Island in the neck of Seaton Sluice harbour and a fine coastal path which threads its way through the dunes north of Seaton Sluice as far as Gloucester Lodge Farm. The inland leg of this loop passes close to Delaval Hall National Trust property. The route is pleasantly rural and provides a shorter variation of Route 30. In summary, this loop packs a lot into it and can be enjoyed on several levels. With so much to stimulate the eye and the mind, it's far more than a cycle loop. Best to ride it for the first time on a sunny day and it will become a firm favourite. Don't forget to take the short detour to St Mary's Island lighthouse when the tide is out and it is safe to cross.

ROUTE NOTES:

1. Eve Black Seaton Sluice dunes path can be busy with pedestrians at peak times and holidays.
2. TAKE CARE when crossing the A193 near Gloucester Lodge Farm.
3. TAKE CARE when crossing the A190 at The Avenue near Seaton Delaval Hall.
4. Whitley Bay promenade path can be busy with pedestrians at peak times and holidays.
5. Check the tide times for a safe crossing to St. Mary's Island.

LOOS & BREWS:

plenty of options on coastal leg but none inland.
Whitley Bay seafront – public houses, restaurants, cafés, shops / WC
Seaton Sluice – public houses, restaurants, cafés / WC

115

Map annotations

- Popular horse-riding route especially at weekends – always give way
- ② TAKE CARE when crossing the A193 near Gloucester Lodge Farm
- ① Cycle considerately and always give way to walkers
- START/END
- ③ TAKE CARE when crossing the A190 The Avenue near Delaval Hall

© Crown copyright 2016 OS Licence 100056069

Scale

STATUTE MILES: -1, 0, 1, 2
KILOMETRES: -1, 0, 1, 2, 3

Route details

Total distance	17 km
Total ascent /descent	40 metres

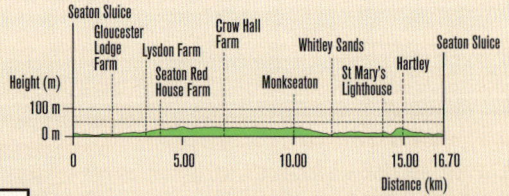

Elevation profile

Labels along profile: Seaton Sluice, Gloucester Lodge Farm, Lysdon Farm, Seaton Red House Farm, Crow Hall Farm, Monkseaton, Whitley Sands, St Mary's Lighthouse, Hartley, Seaton Sluice

Height (m): 0 m, 100 m
Distance (km): 0, 5.00, 10.00, 15.00, 16.70

Not many people know that...

on 1723 Admiral George Delaval, aged 55, died after falling from his horse and the spot is marked by an uninscribed obelisk. Its base still stands by the T-junction to New Harley on The Avenue – the road running past Delaval Hall. The large obelisk behind the hall was built purely as a folly and is often mistaken for the place of his death.

START/END

Seaton Sluice

Check the tide times for a safe crossing to St. Mary's Island

⑤

St Mary's Island

Alternative START/END

Cycle considerately and always give way to walkers

④

WHITLEY BAY
Whitley Sands

Whitley Bay

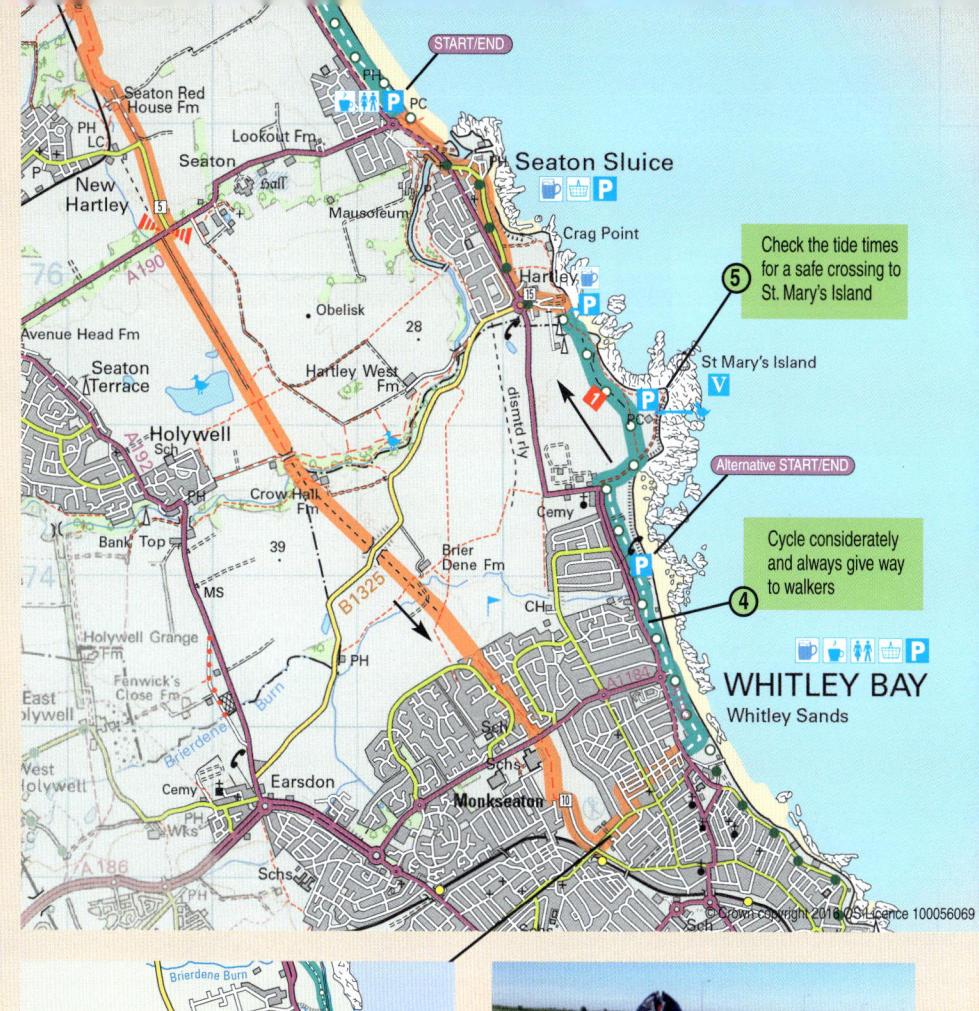

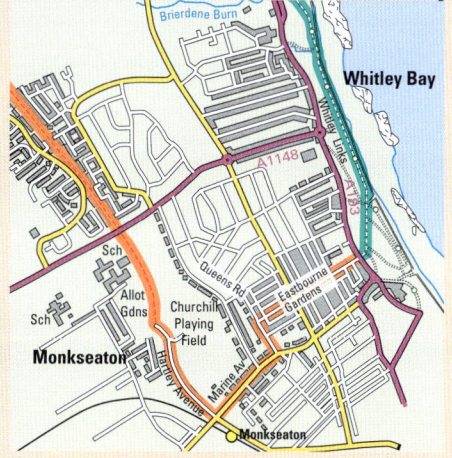

Monkseaton

The Eve Black Way dunes path north of Seaton Sluice.

117

Waggonways & Bridleways 32

Blyth beach huts

Blyth & Seaton Sluice Loop

DISTANCE: 27.5 km / 17.2 miles

GRADE: Easy

START/END
Seaton Sluice, The Links
FREE PARKING: Fountains Head car park, Seaton Sluice and South Beach, Blyth

Alternative START/END
Bedlington
FREE PARKING: Furnace Bank car park near Bedlington

VISITOR INFORMATION
www.seaton-sluice.btck.co.uk
www.blythtown.net

Ordnance Survey maps:
Explorer 325 – Morpeth & Blyth
Explorer 316 – Newcastle-upon-Tyne
Landranger 81 – Alnwick & Morpeth
Landranger 88 – Newcastle-upon-Tyne

Family-friendly section

SUMMARY: *The Blyth & Seaton Sluice Loop* combines a coastal strip of south-east Northumberland with an inland rural experience.

Starting at Seaton Sluice Fountain Head car park, a most enjoyable shared-use path signed *Coasts & Castles Cycle Route* (NCN Route 1), snakes its way through the dunes past Gloucester Lodge Farm, as far as South Beach. Route 1 signing and waymarking is followed around Blyth, first along Links Road, then passing through Ridley Park, to hug soon the side of the River Blyth by the quayside, before picking its way along to the north of the town. In no time, the loop passes through semi-rural scenery, all the while staying close to the narrowing but still tidal River Blyth. A short ascent leads to the dog-leg crossing of the A193 to access Hathery Lane, an old road leading to a bridge over the A186 to pass by Low Horton Farm. The ensuing good bridleway links are surviving evidence of old waggonways, which at one time served the many pits in the area. After an almost direct crossing of the A1061, a very pleasant, tree-covered waggonway leads to Lysdon Farm after the railway underbridge. Cycle around the farm, then through Seaton Red House farm to ride a short section of road before crossing The Avenue. Turn left on the roadside cycle path and next right on to good bridleways that link to Hartley West Farm, before descending the slope into Holywell Dene. All that remains is the short road ascent to Old Hartley and the quiet road next to Collywell Bay to return to Seaton Sluice.

ROUTE NOTES:

① Eve Black Seaton Sluice dunes path can be busy with pedestrians at peak times and holidays.

② Follow NCN Route 1 signs and waymarks through Blyth.

③ **TAKE EXTRA CARE** when crossing A1061 and A190 The Avenue.

LOOS & BREWS:

plenty options on the coastal leg.
Inland leg – near Low Horton Farm,
Three Horse Shoes – 01670 822410 – www.threehorseshoes-horton.co.uk

118

Follow *Coasts & Castles Cycle Route* (NCN Route 1) signs and waymarks through Blyth
Follow signs and waymarks for NCN 1
Cycle considerately and always give way to walkers
Alternative START/END
START/END
START/END
N
BLYTH
North Blyth
The Rockers
Green Skeer
Crab Law
LB Station
Sow and Pigs
Seaton Sea Rocks
South Beach
Link Ho
Gloucester Lodge Fm
Dunes
Mile Hill
Lysdon Fm
Seaton Red House Fm
Lookout Fm
Seaton
New Hartley
North Moor Fm
Stickley Fm
Laverock Hall
New Delaval
Newsham
Low Horton Fm
Bebside Hall
Bebside
Cowpen
Crem
Hospital
Kitty Brewster Fm
Ind Est
Mount Pleasant Fm
Bedlington Station
East Sleekburn
dismantled railway
Cemy
A 189
A193
A192
A1061
© Crown copyright 2016 OS Licence 100056069

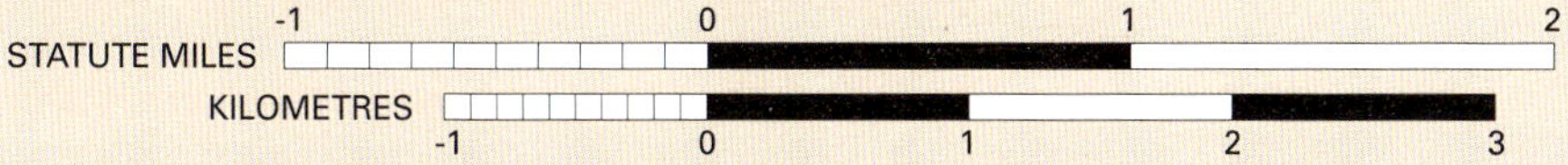
STATUTE MILES
-1
0
1
2
KILOMETRES
-1
0
1
2
3

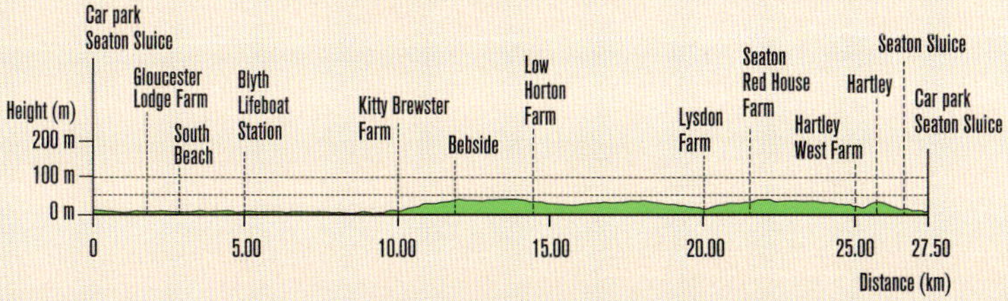
Car park Seaton Sluice
Gloucester Lodge Farm
South Beach
Blyth Lifeboat Station
Kitty Brewster Farm
Bebside
Low Horton Farm
Lysdon Farm
Seaton Red House Farm
Hartley West Farm
Hartley
Seaton Sluice
Car park Seaton Sluice
Height (m)
200 m
100 m
0 m
0
5.00
10.00
15.00
20.00
25.00
27.50
Distance (km)

Follow signs and waymarks for *Coasts & Castles Cycle Route* (NCN Route 1)

Cycle considerately and always give way to walkers

Take care when crossing A190 The Avenue near Delaval Hall

Total distance	27.5 km
Total ascent /descent	157 metres

© Crown copyright 2016 OS Licence 100056069

Not many people know that ... the place-name 'Seaton Delaval' was first attested as 'Seton de la Val' in 1270. 'Seaton' simply means 'sea town', referring to the village's proximity to the North Sea. The land was held by the Delaval family who took their name from Laval in France. The 18th-century Delavals are noted for magnificent Seaton Delaval Hall, now managed by the National Trust and for the development of the little seaport of Seaton Sluice, as well as a coal mine at Old Hartley. Their descendants are still living.

On the route near New Hartley

Waggonways & Bridleways 33

On the riverside path, Wansbeck Riverside Country Park, Ashington

Ashington & River Wansbeck Loop

DISTANCE: 16.6 km / 10.3 miles

GRADE: Easy

START/END
Wansbeck Riverside Country Park
FREE PARKING: Wansbeck Riverside Country Park

Family-friendly sections

SUMMARY: *The Ashington & River Wansbeck Loop* provides a very pleasant circuit of Ashington with surprisingly little on-road traffic. Assuming a start at the west end of the loop at the Riverside Park, right next to the River Wansbeck, the north bank path parallels the river almost to its mouth before it cuts up into and through Sandy Bay Caravan Park and on to the verge cycle path, adjacent to the road into Newbiggin. The next right slips down towards Spital Point and a short slope by a small car park links on to a one-way street overlooking Newbiggin Bay, where a zig-zag leads to a short section of the main road into Newbiggin. Turn left at the ice-cream parlour and head inland along the cycle path (NCN Route 155) to pass under the A189 and the cycle path to Woodhorn. An old, mainly traffic-free road links to an access point for the Queen Elizabeth II Country Park and the path around the lake to slip on to the cycle path next to the A197. Follow this passing through waymarked residential streets, before cycling down the road leading past Ashington Farm. A short section of Green Lane connects to the access road into Riverside Park and completes the loop.

Alternative START/END
Queen Elizabeth Country Park
FREE PARKING: Queen Elizabeth II Country Park

VISITOR INFORMATION
www.visitnorthumberland.com/ashington
www.experiencewoodhorn.com

Ordnance Survey maps:
Explorer 325 – Morpeth & Blyth
Landranger 81 – Alnwick & Morpeth

LOOS & BREWS:
Queen Elizabeth II Country Park
Newbiggin-by-the-Sea: Café Indulgence coffee shop
Ashington: wide choice

Cliff-top view of Newbiggin Bay

121

122

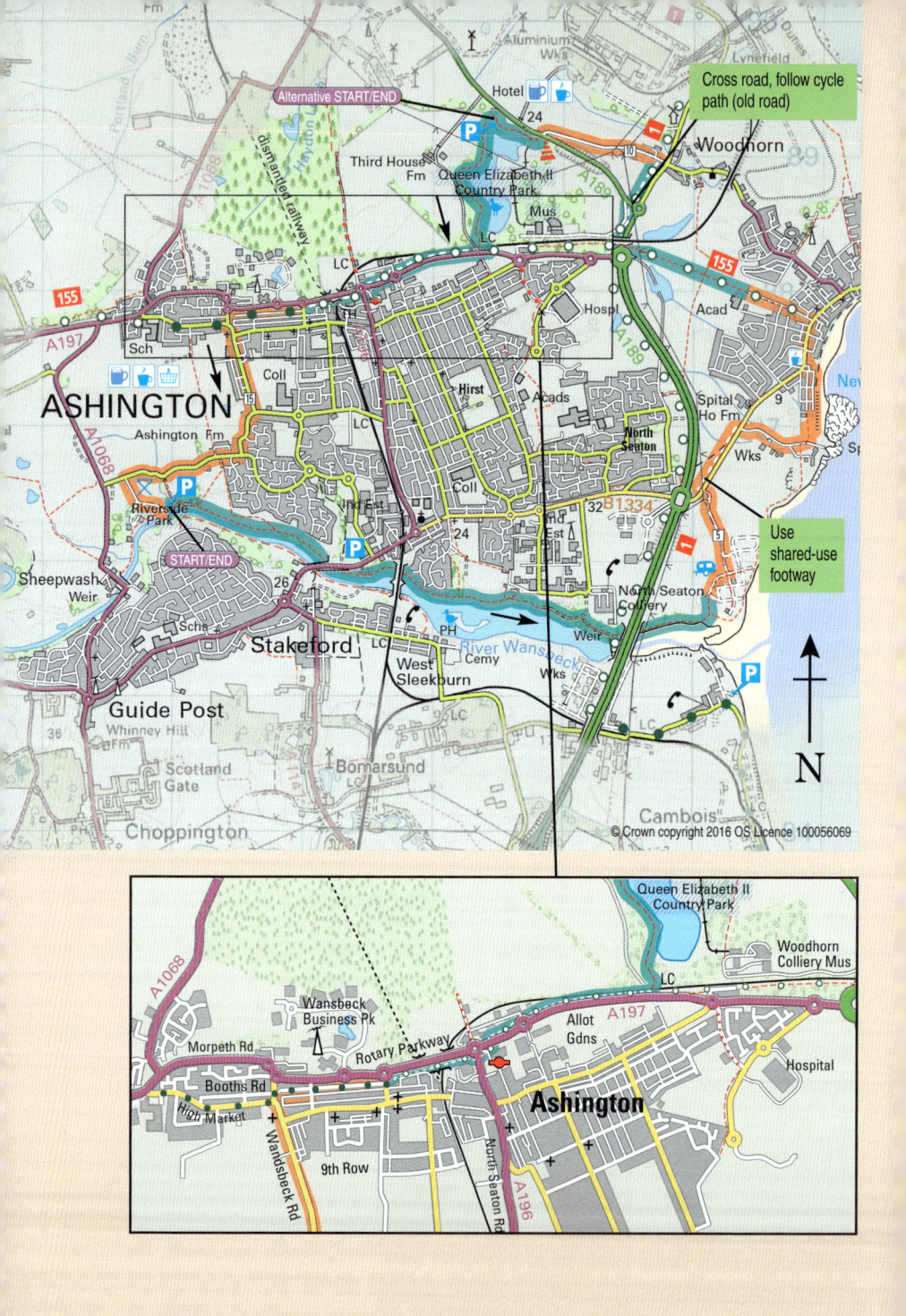

Not many people know that . . . many inhabitants of Ashington have a distinctive accent and dialect known as "Pitmatic". This varies from the regional dialect known as Geordie. It developed as a separate dialect from Northumbrian and Geordie partly due to the specialised terms used by the mineworkers in the local coal pits.

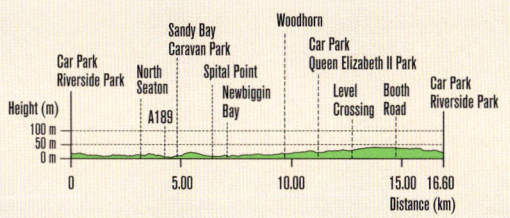

Total distance	16.6 km
Total ascent /descent	353 metres

123

Other maps in the range
Cycle Touring map of Northumberland

Sandstone Way Map – 120 mile mountain bike route between Berwick-upon-Tweed & Hexham

New book coming soon
33 Excellent Mountain Bike Routes in Northumberland & Beyond

Cheviot Hills Map – 12 mountain bike day loop routes. One and two day challenging orbital routes. Two seperate north and south loops.

New
Reivers Cycle Route Map – Updated official map of the Reivers Cycle Route from Tynemouth to Maryport. The route consists of two versions - a 100% tarmac route for all types of bikes. and a version which, as much as possible is off-road suitable for gravel bikes, hybrids and mountain bikes.

Available from: www.northern-heritage.co.uk

ROUTE NOTES

ROUTE NOTES

ROUTE NOTES

ROUTE NOTES

Photo: © Andy McCandlish/www.andymccandlish.com

Enjoy!
cycling Northumberland